Gingermelon's
EMBROIDERED
ANIMALS

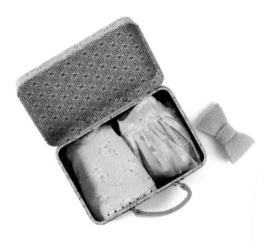

Heirloom animal dolls to sew,
embellish and treasure

SHELLY DOWN

www.sewandso.co.uk

CONTENTS

INTRODUCTION

For this book, I've created an adorable collection of stuffed animal dolls, each with unique, hand-embroidered facial details and an outfit to complete the look. With the exception of the ears, which reflect each of the animals' individual characters, the pattern to make the basic doll will enable you to make all the dolls, as it is the same for all the projects in the book. Each animal character is created with fabric and a combination of hand and machine sewing techniques are used to complete it.

I've also designed a collection of fun outfits, which can be mixed and matched to create a wonderfully diverse wardrobe for your dolls.

HOW THIS BOOK WORKS

I have designed the projects in this book to be fun and easy to make and have provided simple, easy-to-follow patterns, instructions and lots of step-by-step illustrations to guide you along the way, so that even a beginner sewer will enjoy making them! I've used a variety of different types of fabric to make the dolls and their outfits, which include medium-weight cotton and cotton blends for the dolls' bodies, and lightweight cottons and cotton blends such as lawn and double gauze for their outfits. Some novelty/specialty fabrics such as faux fur, teddy fur, tulle, lightweight suede or velour and wool felt were also used for some of the projects. A variety of easy hand embroidery stitches are used on the dolls, with instructions on how to sew them in the Stitch Guide. The finished dolls measure about 30.5cm (12in) tall and are perfect for snuggles and sharing secrets and dreams with!

TOOLS AND MATERIALS

In order to make the projects in this book, you'll need a few basic sewing supplies and tools to get you started. Most of these items should be available at your local fabric or craft supply store and there are many online websites that carry a wide range of fabric and supplies as well.

ESSENTIAL SUPPLIES

FABRIC

I've chosen to use a medium-weight cotton to make most of the dolls in this book, with the exception of the unicorn, which has been made with a lightweight, satin-backed suede (which I re-purposed from a cushion cover!). It's fun to get creative and with a little imagination, you can turn vintage linen, second-hand clothing or household items into brand new creations! Here are some ideas for fabric you may want to consider using for making your doll.

- Medium-weight cotton or cotton blends in solid colours such as ColorWorks Premium Solid 9000, Peppered Cottons by Pepper Cory, muslin, and so on for the doll's main body.

- Lightweight cottons such as Liberty of London, double gauze, sheeting, lawn, and so on for the outfits.

- Fabrics such as satin, flannel, velour, velvet, or baby corduroy. These fabrics would work well to create the dolls, or to use as accents for making the inner ears, unicorn's horn, owl's feathers and inner wings and so on.

- For some of the projects, I've used novelty fabrics such as faux fur for the unicorn's mane and the deer's cape, teddy fur for the lamb's forehead and outer ears, lightweight suede for the unicorn's body and head, tulle to make the elephant's tutu and sparkly glitter netting to make the owl's skirt overlay.

EMBROIDERY THREAD (FLOSS)

Embroidery thread is available in most needlecraft stores and comes in a wide array of colours, finishes and weights. I have used a combination of cotton and metallic embroidery threads from DMC and Lecien Cosmo to create the hand-embroidered details on my dolls. Cotton threads are made from high quality, extra-long staple cotton, which is known for its strength and durability, and because it's been double mercerized, it produces a brilliant sheen. These threads are easy to work with and are suitable for use on all types of fabric.

Cotton embroidery thread is usually comprised of six strands of thread, which are easily separated and allow you to adjust the thickness of your stitching simply by changing the number of strands used. For most of the projects in this book, unless otherwise stated, just one strand of thread is needed for embroidering the facial features and the unique embroidered design on each animal. I've used four main types of embroidery thread for the projects.

- DMC Cotton embroidery thread.

- DMC Satin embroidery thread.

- DMC Light Effects thread (metallic).

- Lecien Cosmo Nishikiito Metallic thread.

TRIMS

Trims are mainly used to add detail to the dolls' outfits and there are many different types to choose from. To keep the look of these dolls simple and dainty, I've mostly used narrow cotton lace, tiny pompom trim and narrow ribbon.

SCISSORS

I find it helpful to have a couple of pairs of scissors on hand for completing projects. The first is a pair of good quality dressmaking scissors (or my personal favourite, a pair of pinking shears) and the second is a pair of embroidery scissors.

DRESSMAKING SCISSORS OR PINKING SHEARS

Investing in a pair of good quality dressmaking scissors or pinking shears is well worth the expense. There are many exceptional brands to choose from, such as Fiskars, Kai and Gingher, and with a little research you should be able to find a pair that suits you perfectly. A good pair of scissors will glide through fabric accurately and smoothly regardless of the weight of the fabric and should also be comfortable to handle. Not only will a good pair of scissors last you a lifetime, they will also retain their sharpness much longer than lesser quality ones.

EMBROIDERY SCISSORS

Perfect for delicate work, the long, slender blades of a classic pair of stork embroidery scissors are ideal for embroidery and needlework projects. They are also wonderful for cutting out smaller pieces of fabric and felt.

NEEDLES AND PINS

It's important to use pins and needles with sharp tips, as using blunt ones could leave holes in the fabric that don't disappear easily. I tend to prefer using thinner pins and needles for my dollmaking as they're easier to insert into the fabric. Apart from general needles, here are some of my favourites.

NEEDLES

- Tulip – bead embroidery sharps #10 short.

- John James – long and short beading needles.

- Unique Doll Needles – extra-long, thin needles used to attach doll arms.

PINS

- Dritz – ultra-fine glass-headed pins, size 22, 3.5cm (1⅜in).

- Unique Pearl Head Hat pins – these pins are extra-long, very strong and great for pinning the doll's head onto the neck. I also like to use them for pinning the arms onto the sides of the body.

EMBROIDERY HOOP

A wooden hoop about 12.5cm (5in) in diameter will work perfectly for these projects. Place the fabric between the two hoops and adjust the screw to tighten the outer hoop and keep the fabric taut. Keeping fabric taut makes it easier to embroider the design.

STUFFING AND STUFFING TOOLS

There are many types of stuffing available, ranging from natural to synthetic fibres. I prefer to use Fairfield Ultra Plush Super Soft Polyester Fiber Fill, as it's lovely and soft and holds its shape well.

The best stuffing tools are items that you probably already have at hand. A wooden spoon is perfect for pushing stuffing into larger areas, while a chopstick or orange stick (cocktail stick) are great for stuffing smaller areas. For very small areas, I like to cut off one end of a cotton bud (Q-tip) and use the cut end for stuffing these extra tiny areas. Alternatively, a sturdy flat toothpick also works nicely. A narrow plastic drinking straw will come in handy for aiding in turning narrow pieces, such as arms and legs and shoulder straps. Cut one end off a narrow plastic straw on a 45-degree angle, and then insert the angled side of the straw into the opening of the piece to be turned. Then insert an orange stick or chopstick into the sewn edge of the fabric at the end of the straw. Gently push the stick down into the straw, being careful not to push the stick through the stitches. Remove the straw and then use the orange stick to gently push out the corners.

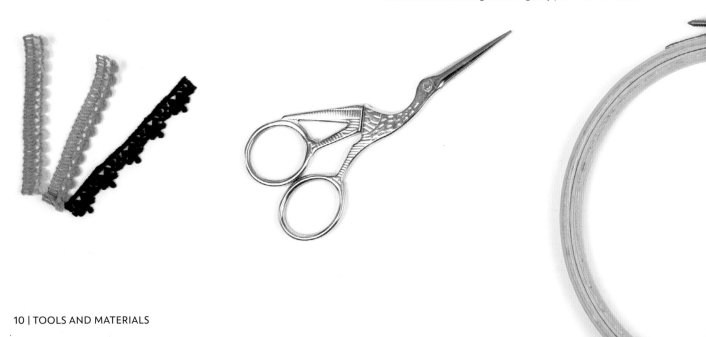

FINE-POINT DISAPPEARING-INK MARKER

This pen is ideal for transferring pattern markings and embroidery designs onto fabric. I use one made by Dritz. The ink vanishes over time, but it can also be refreshed by gently pressing the fabric with a warm iron. To make the markings disappear faster, lightly dab the area with a cotton bud (Q-tip) soaked in water – the ink will instantly darken, but as it dries it will disappear completely.

OTHER SUPPLIES

BEADS, SEQUINS AND FLAT-BACKED CRYSTALS

Widely available in many colours and finishes, these little notions are wonderful for adding details to your projects.

SNAP CLOSURES

Snap closures, also known as press studs, pops or snaps, are used for fastening clothing. They consist of a pair of interlocking discs made out of metal or plastic, which when closed, stay locked together until a certain amount of force is applied to prise them apart. One side of the disc has an indent (female) and the other side has a raised nub (male).

SAFETY EYES AND CONNECTORS

The eyes on the dolls in this book are embroidered but you may want to make the toys using safety eyes. Safety eyes or craft eyes are available in different sizes and colours and are used mainly for handmade plush toys and amigurumi. They consist of two parts, a plastic front (eye) with a smooth, straight or threaded post and a plastic or metal washer that fits onto the back of the post. If using safety eyes, you will also need an awl and some wire cutters. An awl is handy for piercing eye holes, while the wire cutters are useful for trimming back the posts of the safety eyes once they've been inserted.

RULER

An ordinary plastic or wooden ruler is useful for connecting the drawn grid lines as you prepare the fabric to embroider the facial details on a doll's head.

FRAY CHECK™

Fray Check liquid can be found at most fabric shops and is a type of clear-drying glue used to help prevent fabric from fraying at the edges. Run a small bead of Fray Check along the cut edge of fabric, ribbon, lace trim or seam binding to prevent the edges from fraying.

CLEAR-DRYING CRAFT GLUE

Used for sticking the flat-backed crystals onto Darling Ellie's ballet top.

PINK PENCIL

A good quality, pink-coloured pencil is essential for creating rosy cheeks on the dolls. I like to use the pink (PC929) from Prismacolor Premier, as it has a rich, highly saturated pigment that works well on fabric and felt. It's available in a set or sold individually in craft stores.

PAPER

Trace the pattern pieces from the book onto regular computer printer paper before cutting them out. Please be sure to label the pattern pieces with the correct labels so that you can keep them organized.

WASHI TAPE

This tape is useful for attaching a pattern to a bright window, so it can be traced onto fabric. A 5mm (¼in) width should be fine.

THE
Basic Doll

All the dolls are made from the same basic pattern, except for their ears. I've used a combination of fabrics, ranging from medium-weight cotton for the bodies, to lightweight cotton and cotton blends for the outfits. Each animal's facial features are hand embroidered. Once the embroidery is complete, the head, body, arms, legs and all of the outfits are machine sewn.

YOU WILL NEED

- Sewing supplies: dressmaking scissors, pinking shears, embroidery scissors, pins, general needles, long doll needle and beading needle
- Sewing machine and threads to match fabrics
- Stuffing (fiber fill)
- Turning and stuffing tools, such as wooden spoon, orange stick/chopstick and plastic drinking straws in various widths
- Erasable marker, such as a disappearing-ink marker or water-soluble ink marker
- School ruler
- Embroidery hoop 12.5cm (5in) diameter
- Two pieces of cotton fabric for doll's head, each about 18cm (7in) square
- 23cm x 15cm (9in x 6in) cotton fabric for body
- 23cm x 28cm (9in x 11in) cotton fabric for arms and legs
- For the facial features embroidery:
  DMC Cotton embroidery thread (floss): black (310) for eyes and eyebrows; DMC Satin embroidery thread: white (S5200) for highlights; Lecien Cosmo Nishikiito Metallic thread: copper (16) for snout
- Pink pencil and a cotton bud (Q-tip) for blushing cheeks
- Washi tape 5mm (¼in) wide (for fixing pattern to a window)

HAND EMBROIDERY STITCHES USED

Refer to the Stitch Guide chapter for these stitches.

- Ladder stitch
- Satin stitch
- Stem stitch
- Straight stitch

LAYOUT AND CUTTING

1 Make a photocopy or trace the pattern pieces for the basic doll onto paper. The patterns are given full size, so there is no need for re-sizing. Cut out each paper pattern piece. Note: the patterns do not include seam allowances, as most of the pieces are traced onto the fabric with a fabric marker and then stitched on the traced lines. The fabric shapes are then cut out with 5mm (¼in) seam allowance, cut by eye. Refer to each project for full instructions. The final shape of the head will depend on how the pattern piece is placed on the grain of the fabric. The warp thread, generally the stronger thread, runs up and down (vertically) along the fabric, while the weft thread, which has a bit of stretch, runs right to left (horizontally). I have chosen to lay the pattern pieces onto the fabric so that the arrows on the pattern follow the direction of the fabric warp grain, so follow the directions of the arrows printed on each paper pattern piece.

2 Trace the head pattern piece onto the right side of one of the 18cm (7in) squares of fabric with a disappearing-ink marker. To mark the grid on the head, keep the head pattern piece pinned in place and gently lift the outer edges. Use the marker to mark the beginning of the lines onto the fabric. Now remove the pattern piece and use a ruler to connect the lines (Fig 1). This grid will help with the placement of the facial features.

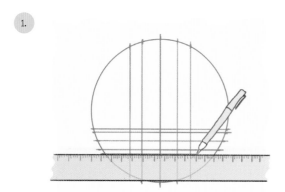
1.

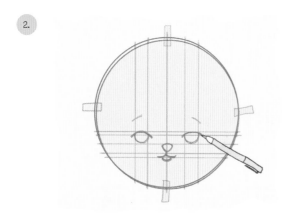
2.

3 To transfer the facial markings and embroidered design for the animal you've chosen to make, use washi tape to fix the paper head pattern piece onto a window, so the light shines through the pattern. Alternatively, tape the pattern piece onto a light box. Now tape the fabric onto the window over the paper pattern, making sure to align the horizontal and vertical lines on the paper pattern with the lines you've drawn on the fabric. Use a disappearing-ink marker to trace the facial markings and embroidery design onto the fabric (Fig 2).

4 Remove the fabric from the window/light box and position it over the inside ring of the embroidery hoop, centring the fabric before positioning the outer hoop. Twist the screw at the top of the hoop until the fabric is snug.

EMBROIDERING THE FACIAL FEATURES

1 Whenever a stitch is mentioned, refer to the Stitch Guide chapter for details on how to work the stitch. Begin each animal by following the steps below to embroider their facial features, then use the chapter pertaining to the animal you're making to find the remainder of the instructions and step-by-step illustrations for the animal's unique embroidered design. The individual chapters have instructions on how to make and attach the ears, and also how to make the clothes.

For the embroidered motifs on each animal's head, I have used a variety of different DMC embroidery threads, ranging from DMC Cotton thread to DMC Satin thread and DMC Light Effects thread. Refer to the specific animal for details. I have also used Lecien Cosmo Nishikiito Metallic thread in some instances (but you could use DMC Light Effects thread instead). Where noted, I have used two or more strands of embroidery thread to embroider the decorative designs onto the head.

I TEND TO USE A SHORT, FINE BEADING
NEEDLE TO STITCH ALL MY EMBROIDERIES,
AS I FIND THAT LARGER NEEDLES TEND
TO MAKE BIGGER HOLES IN THE FABRIC.

2 I prefer to use one strand of embroidery thread to stitch the facial features, as I find that the stitches have a light, delicate finish, whereas using two or more strands can make the details look overly bulky. I used DMC Satin thread in white (S5200) for the eye highlights as it has a lovely reflective sheen, but regular white cotton embroidery thread works just as well.

3 Begin with the eyes. Insert a needle threaded with one strand of black cotton embroidery thread through the back of the fabric and out through the inner corner of the right eye. Using stem stitch, outline the top curve of the eye and then outline the rounded part of the eye. Fill in the rounded part of the eye with satin stitch, working neatly and evenly and keeping stitches close together (Fig 3). Repeat for the left eye. Using black stem stitch, embroider the eyebrows and eyelashes (some dolls do not have eyelashes).

4 Outline the snout in copper metallic (or a brown cotton embroidery thread) with stem stitch (Fig 4). Fill in the centre of the snout with satin stitch, working neatly and evenly and keeping your stitches close together (Fig 5). Using the same thread and stem stitch, embroider the mouth. Add a smudge of pink pencil to the mouth and cheeks.

5 Using white Satin embroidery thread, make a couple of tiny straight stitches in the top right-hand corner of each eye and the top right-hand corner of the snout. This will give the illusion of light reflecting off the eyes and snout.

3.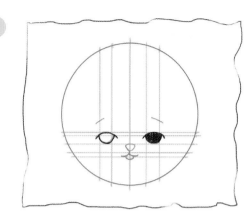

4.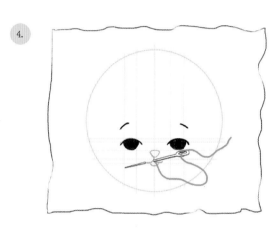

5.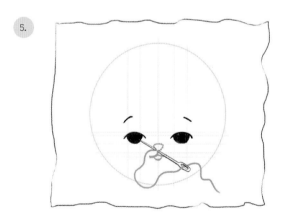

Tip

YOU CAN MIX AND MATCH THE EMBROIDERED MOTIFS FROM MOST OF THE ANIMALS TO CREATE YOUR OWN CUSTOMIZED DOLL. SIMPLY CHOOSE THE MOTIF YOU'D LIKE TO USE AND TRACE IT ONTO THE HEAD FABRIC OF YOUR DOLL, USING THE FACIAL GRID AS A GUIDE FOR PLACEMENT.

ASSEMBLING THE HEAD

1 Remove the head fabric from the embroidery hoop and gently press it flat. The heat from the iron will activate the erasable marker and you should be able to see the traced outline of the head clearly on the fabric. Turn the fabric around so that the back of the head fabric is facing up. You should be able to make out the outline of the head from the right side of the fabric. Place the head paper pattern piece onto the back of the fabric and use a disappearing-ink marker to re-trace the outline of the head onto the wrong side of the fabric, aligning the pattern's outer edges exactly with the outline that you've drawn on the right side. Mark dots at the top of the head for the opening. You do not need to mark the grid on the wrong side of the fabric. Place the head fabric onto the second 18cm (7in) square of fabric, right sides facing, and pin together.

2 Set your sewing machine stitch to straight stitch and use a short stitch length. Place the head onto the bed of the sewing machine and align the needle with the edge of the traced outline at the top of the head where the dot on the right begins (Fig 6). Sew directly on the marked line, starting and ending the seam with a back stitch and leaving a long tail of thread for sewing up the opening later. Trim excess fabric around the head (using pinking shears if you like) and leaving a little tab between the dots for the opening at the top of the head. Turn the head right side out and press (Fig 7).

3 Begin to stuff the head, using a wooden spoon or orange stick/chopstick to push the stuffing down into the lower area of the face. Fill up the bottom of the face, then add stuffing to fill the cheeks, eye area and forehead. Push the stuffing down from the front and back of the head so it is evenly distributed and use your hands to squish and form the shape of the head as you fill it. The head should be nice and full, but not to the point of bursting at the seams. As you get closer to the opening, pin the opening together (Fig 8) and start ladder stitching the area closed, adding more stuffing as you close and rounding out the top part of the head. Pull the thread firmly but not too tightly after a few ladder stitches, as this allows the two sides of the head to close evenly.

6.

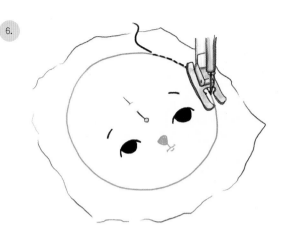

7.

8.

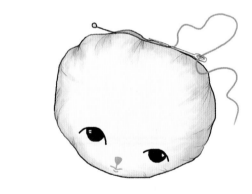

Tip

I PREFER TO USE A DISAPPEARING-INK MARKER. IF AT ANY TIME DURING THE EMBROIDERING PROCESS THE MARKED FACIAL FEATURES HAVE BEGUN TO FADE, GENTLY PRESS A WARM IRON AGAINST THE FABRIC TO REFRESH THE MARKINGS.

Tip

ADD A FEW PINCHES OF CRUSHED, DRIED LAVENDER WHILST ADDING THE STUFFING TO THE BODY. THIS WILL GIVE THE DOLL A LOVELY SOFT SCENT.

ASSEMBLING THE BODY

1 Fold the 23cm x 15cm (9in x 6in) piece of fabric for the body in half widthways, right sides facing. Pin the front body and back body paper pattern pieces onto the fabric (Fig 9). Cut out the pattern pieces. To mark the opening on the back body fabric piece, keep the paper pattern piece pinned in place, gently lift the outer edges and use a disappearing-ink marker to mark the dots for the opening onto the fabric.

2 Remove the paper pattern pieces and pin the fabric pieces together. For the front body, pin along the rounded curve of the body from the dot at A to the dot at B shown on Fig 10. Pin the back body, placing pins between the dots at A and B and between the dots at C and D, as shown.

3 Set your sewing machine stitch to straight stitch and stitch the front body from the dot at A to the dot at B, about 5mm (¼in) away from the edge of the fabric (Fig 11). Back stitch at the beginning and end of the seam and cut off excess thread from both ends. Stitch the back body from A to B. Begin and end the seam with back stitch and leave a long tail of thread at the B dot and cut off excess thread at A. The tail of thread at B will be used to sew up the opening at the back of the body in a later step. Now stitch from the dot at C to the dot at D, again starting and ending the seam with a back stitch and cutting off excess thread at each end. Open the fabric on both front and back body pieces and press the seams flat. Snip the pointed corners at the top and bottom of each seam, so that the edges of the seams match the rounded edges of the top and bottom of the front and back body pieces.

4 Place the front body and back body together, right sides facing and pin (Fig 12). Beginning at the seam at the top narrower end of the body, stitch all the way around the body about 5mm (¼in) away from the fabric edge. Trim excess fabric and snip off corners at the bottom sides of the body.

5 Turn the body right side out and bring the tail of thread out through the opening on the back of the body. You will use this thread for sewing up the opening after the body has been stuffed. Stuff the body firmly, first filling up the bottom and then rounding out the tummy and chest areas. Add stuffing to the neck area, making sure to pack the stuffing firmly (Fig 13). This will provide a good base for attaching the head onto the body later on. Once the body is fully stuffed, begin ladder stitching the opening at the back of the body closed. Add stuffing to fill in the area below the opening as needed. Note: the lamb body could be made out of teddy fur fabric, so see that chapter for instructions.

9.

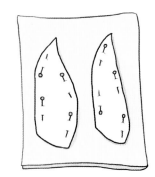

10.

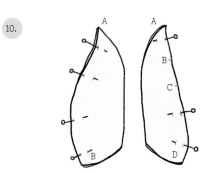

11.

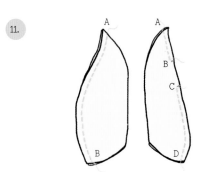

12.

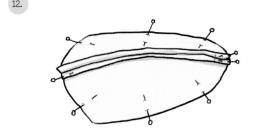

13.

MAKING THE ARMS AND LEGS

1 Fold the 23cm x 28cm (9in x 11in) piece of cotton fabric in half lengthways, right sides together, warp running vertically. Trace the arms and legs paper pattern pieces onto the wrong side of the fabric with a disappearing-ink marker, marking dots for openings along the backs of the arms and the insides of the legs (Fig 14). Pin the fabric together. The seams for each body part are machine stitched directly onto traced outlines of the pattern pieces. Set your sewing machine stitch to straight stitch and use a short stitch length. Stitch directly onto the traced outlines of the pattern pieces, leaving the area between the marked dots open for turning and stuffing and beginning and ending each seam with a back stitch (Fig 15). Leave a long tail of thread for sewing openings later.

2 Trim excess fabric around each piece, leaving a little tab between the dots for the openings near the top of the legs and the back of the arms. Turn each limb right side out using a plastic drinking straw to aid in turning. To do so, insert the straw into the limb and then insert a chopstick/orange stick through the fabric on the outside and into the hole at the top of the straw. Gently push the chopstick/orange stick down into the straw to turn the limb inside out (Fig 16).

3 Stuff the arms and legs, making sure each piece is evenly stuffed (Fig 17). Tuck the tabs in at the back of the arms/top of legs and ladder stitch the openings closed, adding more stuffing to fill in if needed (Fig 18).

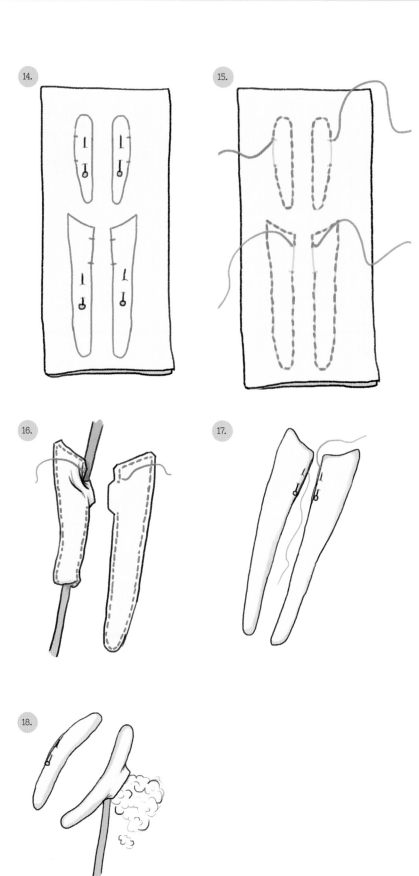

ATTACHING THE HEAD

1 Position the head onto the neck area of the body, matching the head seam with the seams on either side of the body. Pin in place, inserting sturdy pins in through the chest area at the front and the upper area of the back on the back side of the body, up through the neck and into the head (Fig 19).

2 Turn the doll so that the back of the head is facing you. Thread a beading needle with one strand of cotton embroidery thread to match the fabric. Insert the needle along the top seam of the neck, just below the head. Working clockwise around the head, ladder stitch the head onto the neck, keeping your stitches small and neat (Fig 20). Continue ladder stitching around a few more times (an average of five to seven times) to ensure that the head is anchored onto the neck securely. As you stitch the next few rounds, take the ladder stitches a teeny bit lower down on the neck and a teeny bit higher on the face (Fig 21). Keep your stitches tiny and straight, as this will give a nice finish to the seam. End off at the back of the head, tying off the thread along the seam.

19.

20.

21.

Tip

I FIND THAT USING A BEADING
NEEDLE TO ATTACH THE HEAD
ONTO THE NECK HELPS KEEP THE
STITCHES VERY TINY. THIS CREATES
A FINER SEAM AROUND THE HEAD
AND NECK, WHICH LOOKS NEATER
ONCE THE HEAD IS SEWN IN PLACE.

ATTACHING THE ARMS AND LEGS

1 Pin the tops of the legs to the bottom seam of the body (Fig 22). Ladder stitch the front and back of each leg onto the seam (Fig 23).

2 Pin the arms to the sides of the body. Using a double-threaded long doll needle (I like to use embroidery thread), insert the needle underneath one arm, bring it through the body and out through the arm on the opposite side (Fig 24). Make a small stitch and then bring the needle back through the same arm. Go back and forth a few times in this way and then end off under an arm.

MAKING THE EARS

For instructions on how to make and attach the ears please refer to the relevant animal chapter.

FINISHING TOUCHES

To complete your basic doll, use a pink pencil to add a blush of colour to the cheeks. Gently layer the colour onto the cheeks and then use a cotton bud (Q-tip) to smudge the colour in.

IF THE DOLL WILL BE PLAYED WITH BY CHILDREN, BE SURE TO SEW THE ARMS AND LEGS IN PLACE VERY SECURELY. OTHERWISE, LOTS OF HUGS AND KISSES MAY TAKE THEIR TOLL ON WEAK STITCHING.

BASIC DOLL PATTERNS

All the patterns are actual size, so there is no need to enlarge or reduce them. Printable versions of these patterns can be downloaded from: http://ideas.sewandso.co.uk/patterns.

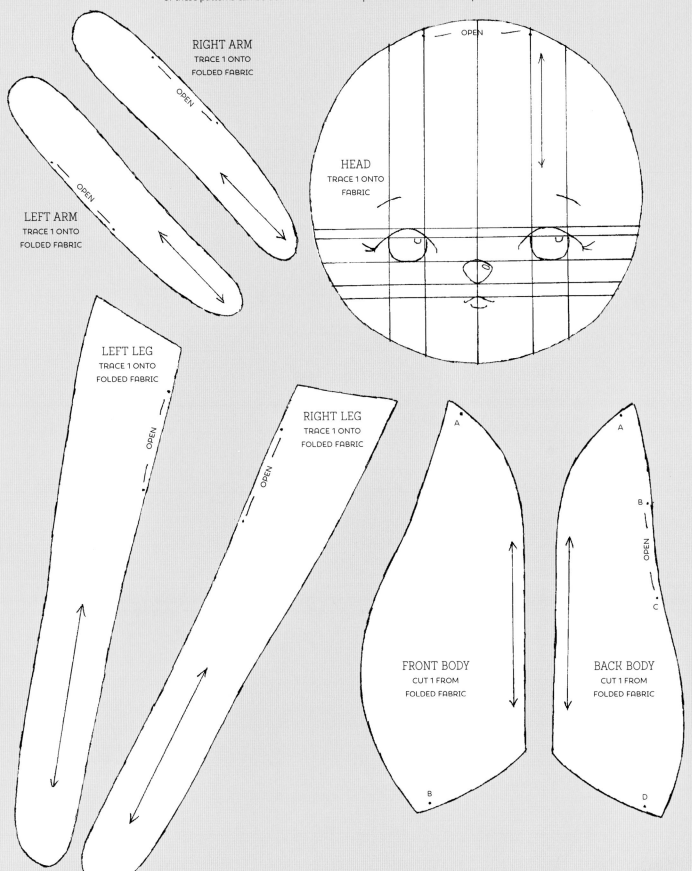

RIGHT ARM
TRACE 1 ONTO
FOLDED FABRIC

OPEN

LEFT ARM
TRACE 1 ONTO
FOLDED FABRIC

OPEN

HEAD
TRACE 1 ONTO
FABRIC

OPEN

LEFT LEG
TRACE 1 ONTO
FOLDED FABRIC

OPEN

RIGHT LEG
TRACE 1 ONTO
FOLDED FABRIC

OPEN

FRONT BODY
CUT 1 FROM
FOLDED FABRIC

A

B

BACK BODY
CUT 1 FROM
FOLDED FABRIC

A

B

OPEN

C

D

FLORAL
Bunny

With her long floppy ears and delicate rose bud embroidery, this sweet little bunny will steal your heart. She wears a pretty floral dress, with matching trim for a special touch. Her cute little bolero jacket is reversible and has a print fabric for the reverse side, so you can give her a new look whenever you like.

YOU WILL NEED

FACE AND ROSES EMBROIDERY

- DMC Cotton embroidery thread (floss): black (310) for eyes and eyebrows, light pink (761), dark pink (760), light yellow (745), moss green (3012) and ecru for roses and leaves
- DMC Satin (or cotton) embroidery thread (floss): white (S5200) for eye and snout highlights
- Lecien Cosmo Nishikiito Metallic thread: copper (16) for snout (or DMC Light Effects thread copper (E301) for a similar look)
- Embroidery needle
- Disappearing-ink marker, ruler and embroidery hoop

HAND EMBROIDERY STITCHES USED

Refer to the Stitch Guide chapter for these stitches.

- Stem stitch
- Satin stitch
- Straight stitch
- Ladder stitch
- Woven wheel stitch
- Lazy daisy stitch
- Whip stitch

MAKING THE BASIC DOLL

Refer to the Basic Doll chapter to make the doll and transfer the head facial features and embroidery motifs onto the bunny's head. Embroider the facial features (eyes and snout) as indicated in the Basic Doll chapter, Embroidering the Facial Features. Embroider eyelashes with stem stitch.

WORKING THE HEAD EMBROIDERY MOTIFS

1 The roses are stitched with four strands of embroidery thread and the leaves with two strands. To make the roses follow the detailed instructions for woven wheel stitch in the Stitch Guide. Begin by threading your needle with four strands of dark pink thread. Embroider the spokes for the base of the rose. Now bring the needle up and out very close to the centre, through the base of one 'V' to begin the weaving stitch to create the petals. Weave the thread over and under each spoke, working in a clockwise direction (Fig 1). Pull the thread gently but firmly so it wraps closely around the centre. Repeat, until half of the length of the spokes are covered.

2 To create the two-tone colour effect on the rose, end off the dark pink thread, switch to four strands of the light pink and continue weaving (Fig 2). Once the spokes are fully covered, angle the needle beneath the flower's woven edge and bring it out through the back of the fabric. End the thread by securing it with a knot.

3 Repeat the process for the yellow rose, stitching the spokes and inner part of the rose with light yellow embroidery thread and finishing the outer petals with ecru thread.

4 To embroider the leaves, thread a needle with a doubled thread of moss green and embroider the leaves with lazy daisy stitch (Fig 3).

5 To complete the head and the rest of the body, refer to the Basic Doll chapter.

1.

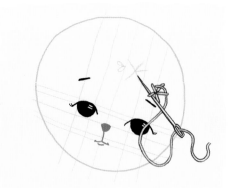

2.

3.

Tip

THE OUTCOME OF THE ROSE WILL DEPEND ON HOW LOOSELY OR TIGHTLY YOU WEAVE YOUR STITCHES. FOR A MORE RAISED, THREE-DIMENSIONAL LOOK, PACK THE WEAVING QUITE TIGHTLY. FOR A FLATTER, MORE OPEN LOOK, KEEP THE WOVEN THREAD LOOSER.

EARS

YOU WILL NEED

- 15cm x 18cm (6in x 7in) cotton fabric for outer ears (to match main body and head)
- 15cm x 18cm (6in x 7in) fabric in pink flannel or cotton for inner ears
- Machine sewing thread to match outer ear fabric
- Straw and chopstick

LAYOUT, CUTTING AND SEWING

1 Place the outer ear and inner ear fabric together, right sides facing. Using a disappearing-ink marker, trace the left and right ear patterns directly onto the cotton fabric, transferring the dots for the opening at the sides of the ears. Pin the pieces together (Fig 4).

2 Stitch around each ear, sewing directly on the marked lines. Begin at one dot at the side of the opening and sew around to the dot on the opposite side, leaving the area between the dots open for turning. Begin and end each seam with a back stitch and leave a long tail of thread once you've reached the dot on the opposite side for sewing the openings closed. Trim excess fabric around each ear, leaving a little tab between the dots for the openings. Clip corners and notch the area between the V at the top of each ear, being careful not to cut into the stitches (Fig 5).

3 To turn the ears right side out, insert a straw into the ear and then insert a chopstick through the fabric on the outside and into the hole at the top of the straw. Gently push the chopstick down into the straw to turn the ear inside out (Fig 6). Tuck the tabs in and ladder stitch the openings closed.

4 Press the ears flat and then fold the top of each ear over so that the sides of the V meet (inner ears on the inside of the fold). Press along the fold and then pin. Thread a needle with matching thread and use small whip stitches to stitch each ear together where the sides of the V meet (Fig 7). Leave a tail of thread for attaching the ears to the head.

5 To attach the ears, put the doll face down on your work area. Position the ears on either side of the head with the inner ears facing upwards. Pin the base of the ears onto the dots marked at the top of the head (Fig 8). When you turn the doll around, the outer ears should be facing up. Ladder stitch the front and back of each ear onto the head seam.

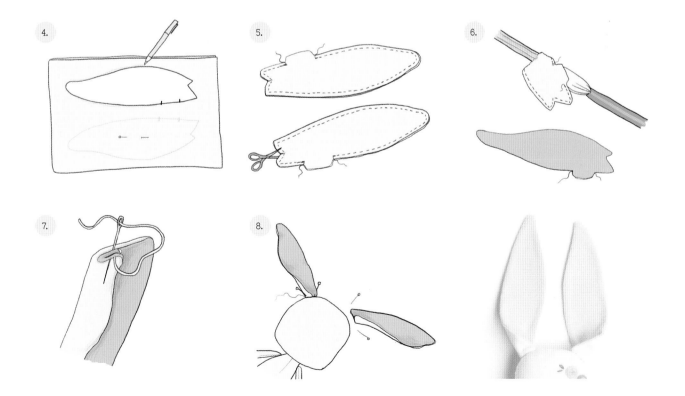

4.

5.

6.

7.

8.

DRESS

- 23cm x 33cm (9in x 13in) lightweight cotton fabric
- Machine sewing thread to match dress fabric and matching or contrasting thread for hem
- Fray Check or fabric glue
- 2cm x 30.5cm (¾in x 12in) long trim for hem
- One 5mm (¼in) snap closure

LAYOUT, CUTTING AND SEWING

1 Fold the 23cm x 33cm (9in x 13in) piece of cotton in half right sides together and place the left-hand side of the dress skirt pattern on the fabric fold. Mark and then cut out with pinking shears. Alternatively, cut out with a pair of dressmaking scissors and zig-zag around the edges with your sewing machine. Fold the short sides of the dress skirt over by about 5mm (¼in) on either side of the skirt, wrong sides facing and pin along the folded edges. Machine sew the folded edges on either side (Fig 9).

2 For the dress bodice, fold the remaining fabric in half widthways, right sides facing. Align the bottom edge of the front of the bodice paper pattern piece along the cut edge. Trace the outline of the bodice directly onto the wrong side of the fabric with a disappearing-ink marker. Pin the fabric together (Fig 10).

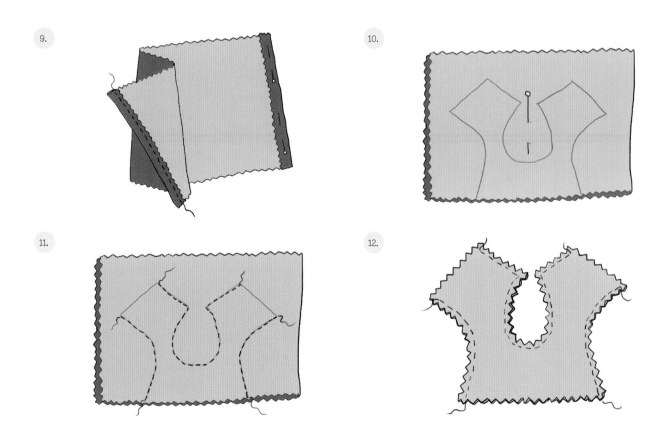

9.

10.

11.

12.

3 Stitch around each armhole, beginning and ending each seam with a back stitch and sewing directly on the marked lines (Fig 11). Stitch up the side of the bodice back, continuing around the neckline and down to the opposite side of the bodice back, beginning and ending the seam with a back stitch and sewing directly on the marked line. Do *not* sew along the opening at the bottom of the front of the bodice, or the areas marked 'Open' on the back of the bodice.

4 Trim excess fabric around the sewn edges of the armholes, back sides and neckline (Fig 12). Turn the bodice right side out, using an orange stick to gently push out the corners. Press flat. Pin the bottom edges together along the front of bodice and then pin the bottom edges of the two back side edges together and machine sew the edges closed with a small zig-zag stitch (Fig 13). Fold the bodice over at the shoulders, matching zig-zagged edges at the front and back, and then pin. Hand stitch a couple of stitches close to the bottom edge on either side to join the front and back together (Fig 14).

5 To attach the bodice to the dress skirt, set your machine stitch on the longest stitch setting (gathering stitch) and sew three rows of gathering stitches about 5mm (¼in) below the top edge of the skirt, leaving long threads on either side for pulling up the gathers later. Fold the dress skirt in half and mark the centre along the top edge on the *right* side of the fabric with a disappearing-ink marker. Repeat the process and mark the centre line at the bottom edge of the inside of the bodice.

6 Match the centre dot on the bottom edge of the bodice with the centre dot on the top edge of the skirt, *right* sides facing and pin at the centre (Fig 15). Pin the left-hand side edge of the bodice to the left-hand side edge of the skirt and then pin the right-hand side edge of the bodice to the right-hand side edge of the skirt. Gently pull the gathers on either side of the skirt until the width of the skirt matches the width of the bodice, pinning along the top edge (Fig 16). To ensure the gathers are even, use a large needle to spread them evenly across the top edge of the skirt.

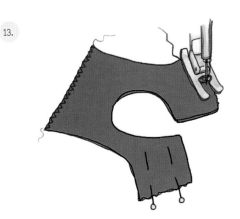

13.

14.

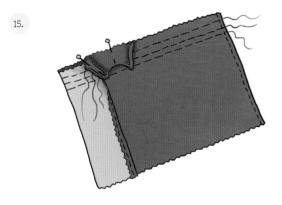

15.

16.

Tip

NOTICE THAT THERE ARE SIX STRANDS OF GATHERING THREADS ON EITHER SIDE OF THE SKIRT. TO ENSURE THAT YOUR GATHERS ARE EVEN, ONLY PULL THE THREE STRANDS OF THE TOP THREADS ON EITHER SIDE OF THE SKIRT.

7 Set your machine stitch on a regular stitch and position the fabric onto the bed of the machine so that the needle is about 5mm (¼in) away from the top edge of the skirt/bodice edge. Stitch the bodice to the skirt (Fig 17). Remove the gathering threads and press the seam up.

8 Fold the bottom edge of the skirt up about 5mm (¼in) and pin. If you'd like to make a simple hem, hand stitch or machine sew the hem in place with matching or contrasting thread (Fig 18). To create a hem with a trim, hand tack (baste) the hem down with one strand of machine thread. For the trim, measure the width of the bottom of the skirt and cut the trim to match. Run a small bead of Fray Check along the trim's cut edges and allow it to dry thoroughly. This will help prevent the ends from fraying. Pin the trim onto the hem on the wrong side of the fabric. Machine or hand sew the trim in place and remove the tacking (basting) stitches (Fig 19).

9 Fit the dress onto the doll and turn it around so that the back of the doll is facing you. Determine where the snap closure should be and mark the area on each side of the bodice with a disappearing-ink marker. Remove the dress and sew the snaps in place (Fig 20).

17.
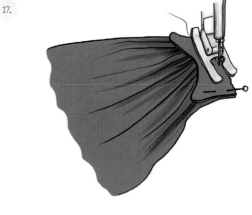

18.
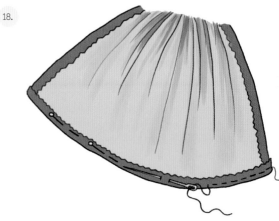

19.
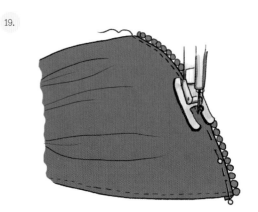

20.

REVERSIBLE BOLERO

- 12.5cm x 18cm (5in x 7in) lightweight cotton fabric in a solid colour
- 12.5cm x 18cm (5in x 7in) lightweight cotton fabric in floral print
- Machine sewing thread to match solid fabric

LAYOUT, CUTTING AND SEWING

1 Place the solid fabric and printed fabric together, right sides facing. Using a disappearing-ink marker, trace the bolero pattern directly onto the fabric, transferring the dots for the opening at the back of the bolero. Pin the pieces together (Fig 21).

2 Place the bolero fabric onto the bed of the sewing machine with the needle aligned on the edge of the traced outline of the jacket at the dot on the right of the opening at the back. Sew directly on the marked line around to the dot on the opposite side at the back, starting and ending your seam with a back stitch and leaving a long tail of thread for sewing up the opening later. Trim excess fabric around the edges, leaving a little tab between the dots for the opening at the back of the bolero (Fig 22). Notch curves around the neck and under the arms and clip off square edges, being careful not to cut into the stitches.

3 Turn the bolero right side out and tuck the tab in at the bottom seam. Pin the edges together, ladder stitch the opening closed and then press. Fold the bolero in half lengthways and pin the sleeves and sides together (Fig 23). Ladder stitch the front and the back of jacket together, joining the sleeves and sides with matching thread.

21.

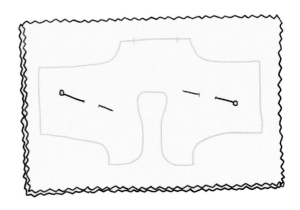

22.

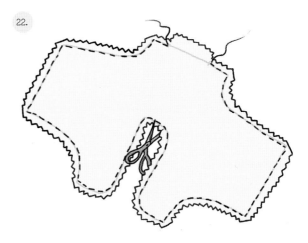

23.

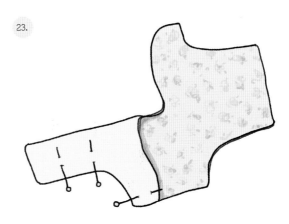

FLORAL BUNNY
PATTERNS

The Bunny also requires the Basic Doll patterns – see end of Basic Doll chapter. All the patterns are actual size, so there is no need to enlarge or reduce them. Printable versions of these patterns can be downloaded from: http://ideas.sewandso.co.uk/patterns.

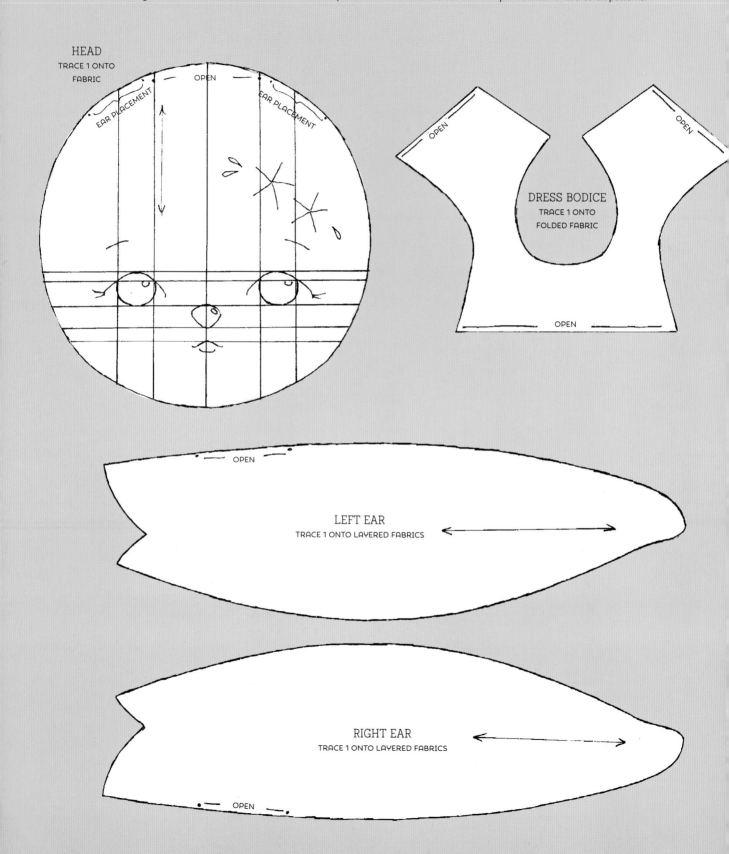

HEAD
TRACE 1 ONTO
FABRIC

OPEN

EAR PLACEMENT

EAR PLACEMENT

OPEN

OPEN

DRESS BODICE
TRACE 1 ONTO
FOLDED FABRIC

OPEN

OPEN

OPEN

LEFT EAR
TRACE 1 ONTO LAYERED FABRICS

RIGHT EAR
TRACE 1 ONTO LAYERED FABRICS

OPEN

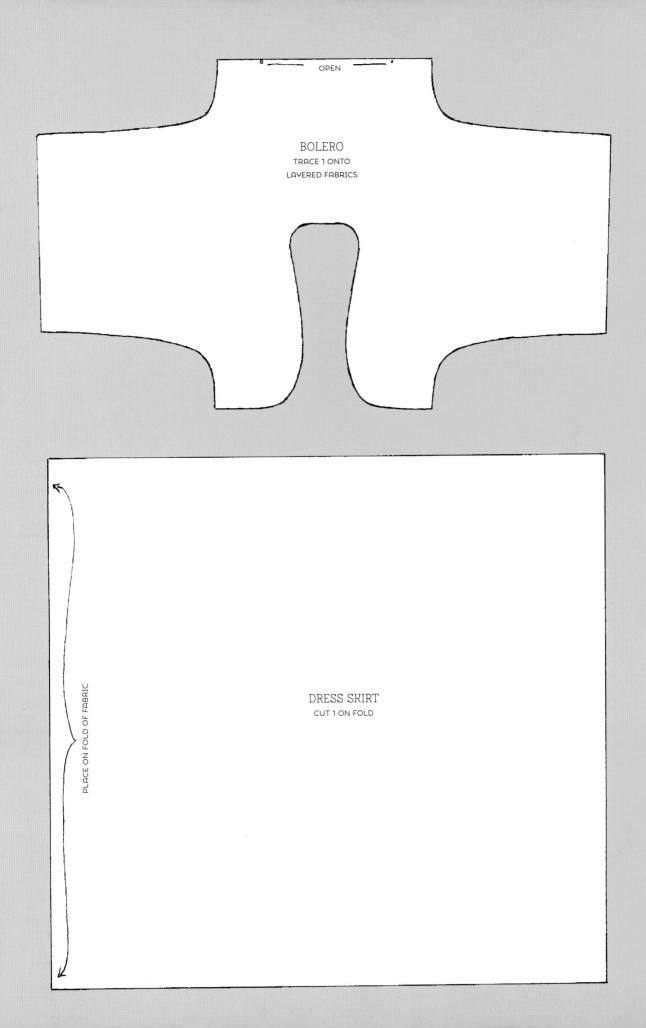

OPEN

BOLERO
TRACE 1 ONTO
LAYERED FABRICS

DRESS SKIRT
CUT 1 ON FOLD

PLACE ON FOLD OF FABRIC

SHOOTING STAR
Kitty

Dressed in a soft floral romper suit complete with a handy pocket to store her little treasures, this adorable pussy cat is ready to take on any adventure! She enjoys playing dress-up and make-believe and loves to snuggle up in front of a crackling fire to read fairy tale books.

YOU WILL NEED

FACE AND STAR EMBROIDERY

- DMC Cotton embroidery thread (floss): black (310) for eyes and eyebrows, navy (3750) and lavender (209) for dashed lines and aqua (964) for French knots
- DMC Satin embroidery thread: white (S5200) for eye and snout highlights (or white Cotton embroidery thread)
- DMC Light Effects thread: silver (E168) for whiskers and purple (E3837) for star
- Lecien Cosmo Nishikiito Metallic thread: copper (16) for snout (or DMC Light Effects thread copper (E301) for a similar look)
- Six rose gold seed beads
- Embroidery needle
- Disappearing-ink marker, ruler and embroidery hoop

HAND EMBROIDERY STITCHES USED

Refer to the Stitch Guide chapter for these stitches.

- Stem stitch
- Satin stitch
- Straight stitch
- French knot
- Ladder stitch

MAKING THE BASIC DOLL

Refer to the Basic Doll chapter to make the doll and transfer the head facial features and embroidery motifs onto the head. Embroider the facial features (eyes and snout) as indicated in the Basic Doll chapter, Embroidering the Facial Features. Outline the mouth with stem stitches and embroider the eyelashes at the outer corner of each eye with stem stitch. All embroidery is done with one strand of thread unless otherwise stated.

WORKING THE HEAD EMBROIDERY MOTIFS

1 To create the shooting star embroidery, sew each curved dashed line with a double row of straight stitches, stitching the first dashed line with navy thread and the second with lavender (Fig 1). Embroider the star with straight stitches and purple Light Effects thread (Fig 2). Detailed instructions for this stitch are given in the Lullaby Lamb chapter (see Working the Head Embroidery Motifs).

2 Continuing with the aqua thread, embroider the French knots onto the dots, winding the yarn around the needle three times for each knot (Fig 3).

3 With long, straight stitches, embroider the whiskers on either side of the face using silver Light Effects thread (Fig 4). Sew rose gold seed beads onto the dots.

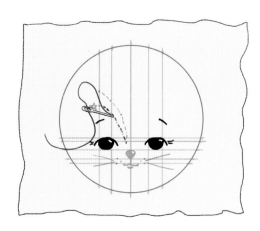

1.

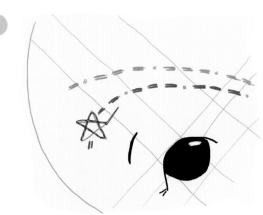

2.

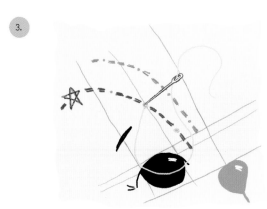

3.

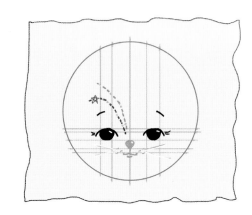

4.

EARS

YOU WILL NEED

- Two pieces 5cm x 10cm (2in x 4in) cotton fabric to match the body
- Matching sewing thread
- Pink pencil

LAYOUT, CUTTING AND SEWING

1 Place the fabrics together, right sides facing. Trace the left and right ear patterns directly onto the fabric with a disappearing-ink marker, transferring the dots for the openings at the base of each ear. Pin the fabrics together (Fig 5).

2 Stitch around each ear, beginning at one dot at the base of the ear and sewing around to the dot on the opposite side, leaving the area between the dots open for turning and stuffing (Fig 6). Begin and end each seam with a back stitch and leave a long tail of thread once you've reached the dot on the opposite side, for sewing the openings closed later. Trim excess fabric around each ear, leaving a little tab between the dots for the openings. Turn the ears right side out and press.

3 To attach the ears to the head, fold each ear slightly and pin each ear onto the marked areas at the top of the head (Fig 7). Ladder stitch the front and back of each ear onto the head seam.

4 To complete the head and the rest of the body, refer to the Basic Doll chapter.

5 Add a hint of colour to the cheeks and the mouth with a pink pencil (Fig 8).

5.

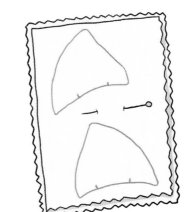

6.

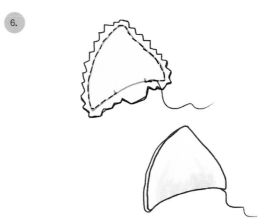

7.

8.

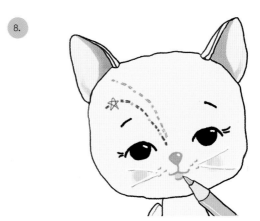

ROMPER SUIT

YOU WILL NEED

- 38cm x 12.5cm (15in x 5in) lightweight floral fabric for pants and straps
- 15cm x 10cm (6in x 4in) lightweight solid fabric for bodice and pocket
- Machine sewing thread to match pants fabric
- Embroidery thread in contrasting colour to attach pocket and straps
- One 5mm (¼in) snap closure
- Straw and chopstick/orange stick
- Fray Check or fabric glue

LAYOUT, CUTTING AND SEWING

1 Pin the romper pants paper pattern piece onto the folded floral fabric and cut out with pinking shears. Separate the two fabric pants pieces (one will be the front and the other the back of the pants) and place them in front of you, wrong sides facing up. Fold the paper pattern piece in half lengthways and place it onto the front pants piece, so that the folded centre of the paper pattern piece is placed along the centre of the fabric and all edges are aligned (Fig 9). Transfer the pattern markings for the inner leg seams onto the fabric. Now place the paper pattern piece onto the back pants piece and transfer the markings for the leg seams and the line running down from the top of the waistband for the opening at the back of the pants. Use a ruler to mark the solid lines in the centre, and then mark the dashed lines running along either side of the centre line. These dashed lines will be the sewing lines.

2 For the romper bodice, fold the 15cm x 10cm (6in x 4in) piece of fabric in half lengthways, right sides facing and trace the outline of the romper bodice directly onto the wrong side of the fabric with a disappearing-ink marker. Pin together. Use pinking shears to cut along the bottom edge of the bodice (Fig 10). Cut out the pocket from left-over fabric. For the shoulder straps, fold the fabric in half lengthways (right sides facing) and place the pattern piece on the fold. Trace the outline of the strap directly onto the wrong side of the fabric. Pin together. Use your pinking shears to cut along the bottom edge of each strap (the open end).

3 Place the front and back of the pants together, right sides facing. Pin the sides together. To create the inner leg seams, position the fabric on the bed of the sewing machine so that the sewing needle is centred at the beginning of one side of the dashed line (running all the way around the centre line) (Fig 11). Stitch directly onto the dashed lines until you get to the other side, beginning and ending the seam with a back stitch. Cut a slit in the centre (solid line), stopping about 5mm (¼in) before the stitches. Notch a tiny V at the top (don't cut into the stitches). Remove the pins from the sides, and press the inner seams open on each leg. Create a hem along the bottom edge of each leg by turning up the fabric about 5mm (¼in), wrong sides facing, and machine sew across (Fig 12).

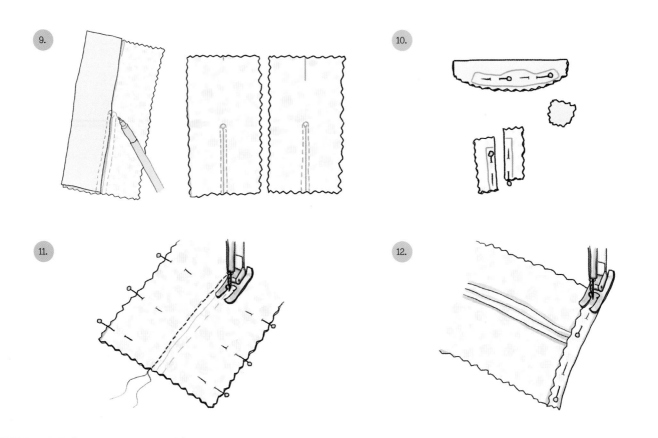

4 With the right sides of the fabric facing, pin the sides together and machine stitch about 5mm (¼in) away from the edges. Before turning the pants right side out, cut a slit for the opening on the back piece with pinking shears (Fig 13). If you're using dressmaking scissors, run a bead of Fray Check around the cut edges and allow to dry thoroughly. Fold the edges of the slit over on each side (wrong sides facing) about 3mm (⅛in) and hand stitch the edges down with contrasting embroidery thread (Fig 14). Keep your stitches neat and small.

5 Set the machine stitch on its longest stitch setting and sew two rows of gathering stitches about 5mm (¼in) below the top edge of the pants, leaving long threads for pulling up the gathers later on (Fig 15). Turn the pants right side out and then mark the centre of the waistband on the front edge.

13.

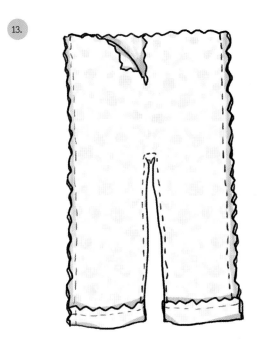

14.

15.

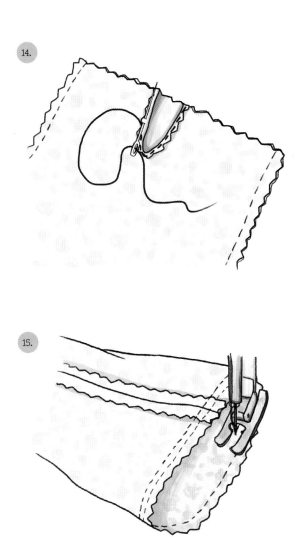

6 To make the romper bodice and straps, start by stitching around the top and sides of the bodice. Trim excess fabric around the sewn edge. Turn the bodice right side out, using an orange stick to gently push out the corners. Press flat and pin the bottom edges together (Fig 16). Stitch around each shoulder strap, leaving the bottom short edge open. Trim excess fabric around the sewn edges. To aid with turning the shoulder straps right side out after sewing, I cut one end of a narrow plastic straw on a 45-degree angle. Insert the angled side into the opening of one strap and then insert an orange stick or chopstick into the edge of the fabric at the end of the straw. Gently push the stick down into the straw. Remove the straw and use the orange stick to gently push out the corners and then press (Fig 17). Machine sew the bottom edges of the bodice and each strap closed with a small zig-zag stitch and then press. Mark the centre of the bodice along the bottom edge with a disappearing-ink marker.

7 To attach the bodice to the pants, match the centre dot on the bottom edge of the bodice with the centre dot on the top edge of the pants, right sides together, and pin at the centre (Fig 18). Working from the left, pin the left-hand side edge of the bodice onto the left-hand side edge of the pants. Repeat on the right side. Gently pull the gathers on both sides of the pants until the width of the pants matches the width of the bodice. To ensure that your gathers are even, use the back of a needle to spread the gathers evenly across the top edge and only pull the top layer of threads from either side (Fig 19). Set the machine stitch on a regular stitch and position the fabric so that the needle is about 5mm (¼in) away from the top edge of the pants. Sew the bodice to the pants. Remove the gathering threads and press the seam down.

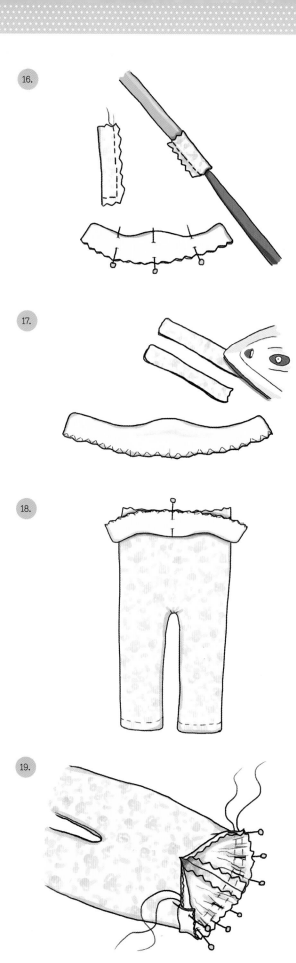

16.

17.

18.

19.

8 Fit the romper suit onto the doll and determine where the snap closure should be at the back of the bodice. Mark the area on each side of the bodice with a disappearing-ink marker and sew the snaps in place (Fig 20).

9 Position the pocket onto the front of the pants and pin in place. Position the sewn edge of one strap onto the front of the bodice, just in front of the arm. Pin in place and repeat with the second strap (Fig 21). Fold the strap over the doll's shoulder and tuck the opposite end of the strap underneath the back side of the bodice. Pin in place and repeat with the second strap (Fig 22). Remove the romper suit and stitch the pocket in place with tiny hand running stitches using a contrasting embroidery thread. Finally, hand sew the straps in place.

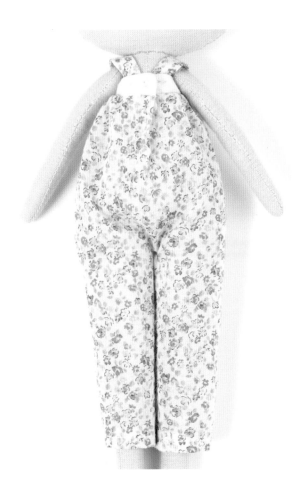

20.

21.

22.

SHOOTING STAR KITTY
PATTERNS

The Kitty also requires the Basic Doll patterns – see end of Basic Doll chapter. All the patterns are actual size, so there is no need to enlarge or reduce them. Printable versions of these patterns can be downloaded from: http://ideas.sewandso.co.uk/patterns.

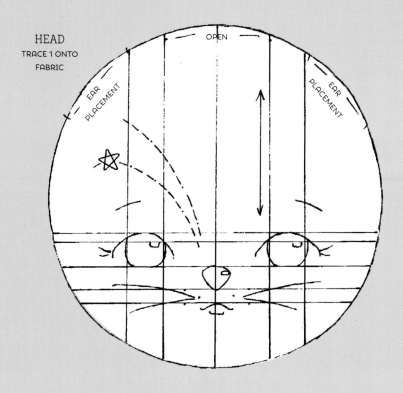

HEAD
TRACE 1 ONTO
FABRIC

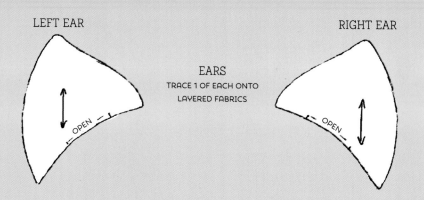

LEFT EAR

RIGHT EAR

EARS
TRACE 1 OF EACH ONTO
LAYERED FABRICS

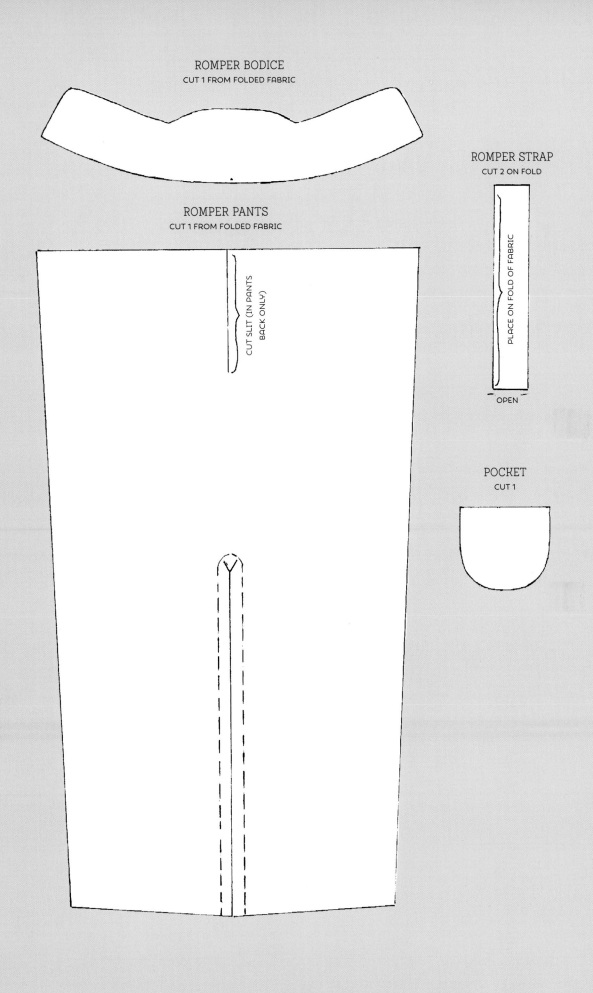

ROMPER BODICE
CUT 1 FROM FOLDED FABRIC

ROMPER STRAP
CUT 2 ON FOLD

ROMPER PANTS
CUT 1 FROM FOLDED FABRIC

CUT SLIT (IN PANTS BACK ONLY)

PLACE ON FOLD OF FABRIC

OPEN

POCKET
CUT 1

WHIMSICAL

Mouse

This shy, sweet little mouse loves tending to her flower garden and watching the butterflies and bees visit her lovely blooms. Her pretty top is made from a lightweight lawn fabric and is paired with breezy capri pants – perfect for a warm day in the sunshine. A tiny felt bow adorns her head and adds a cute finishing touch.

YOU WILL NEED

FACE AND DECORATIVE EMBROIDERY

- DMC Cotton embroidery thread (floss): black (310) for eyes, navy (3750) for floral stems, dark lavender (209) and turquoise (3849) for floral accents, apricot (352) for French knots
- DMC Satin embroidery thread: white (S5200) for eye and snout highlights (or white Cotton embroidery thread)
- DMC Light Effects thread: copper (E301) for lazy daisy stitches below eyes and straight stitches on flower stems
- Lecien Cosmo Nishikiito Metallic thread: pink (12) for snout (or DMC Light Effects thread pink (E316) for a similar look)
- Two small silver seed beads
- Beading needle
- Disappearing-ink marker, ruler and embroidery hoop

HAND EMBROIDERY STITCHES USED

Refer to the Stitch Guide chapter for these stitches.

- Stem stitch
- Satin stitch
- Straight stitch
- Back stitch
- French knot
- Lazy daisy stitch
- Ladder stitch
- Running stitch
- Blanket stitch
- Whip stitch

MAKING THE BASIC DOLL

Refer to the Basic Doll chapter to make the doll and transfer the head facial features and embroidery motifs onto the mouse's head. Embroider the facial features (eyes, eyelashes and snout) as indicated in the Basic Doll chapter, Embroidering the Facial Features. The mouse's facial features are embroidered with one strand of embroidery thread.

WORKING THE HEAD EMBROIDERY MOTIFS

1 The floral embroidery design is stitched with a combination of one and two strands of embroidery thread. Embroider the petals beneath each eye with lazy daisy stitch, using two strands of Light Effects copper thread (Fig 1).

2 Outline the floral stems in back stitch using one strand of navy thread. Using a beading needle, stitch a small bead just above each stem, leaving a tiny space between the end of the stem and the placement of the bead. Insert a needle threaded with one strand of turquoise thread at the top of a stem, just below the bead. Working around the bead and using the marking as a guide, embroider a lazy daisy stitch at the top of the stem (Fig 2). Repeat with the second stem. Using two strands of copper, stitch the straight line across each stem. Using two strands of dark lavender, stitch the lines on either side of the stem, just above the copper stitches (Fig 3).

3 Stitch French knots on either side of the flowers with one strand of apricot, winding the thread around the needle three times to form each knot (Fig 4).

EARS

- 10cm x 7.5cm (4in x 3in) cotton fabric for outer ears, to match main body and head
- 10cm x 7.5cm (4in x 3in) floral cotton fabric for inner ears
- Machine sewing thread to match outer ears
- Straw and chopstick

LAYOUT AND CUTTING

1 Place the outer ear fabric and the inner ear fabric together, right sides facing. Using a disappearing-ink marker, trace the left and right ear patterns directly onto the fabric, transferring the dots for the opening at the base of the ears. Pin the pieces together (Fig 5).

2 Stitch around each ear, beginning at one dot at the base and sewing around to the dot on the opposite side, leaving the area between the dots open for turning. Begin and end each seam with a back stitch and leave a long tail of thread once you've reached the dot on the opposite side. Trim excess fabric around each ear, leaving a little tab between the dots for the openings.

3 Turn the ears right side out using a straw and chopstick. Tuck the tabs in and ladder stitch the openings closed, leaving a tail of thread for attaching the ears to the head (Fig 6). Press the work.

1.

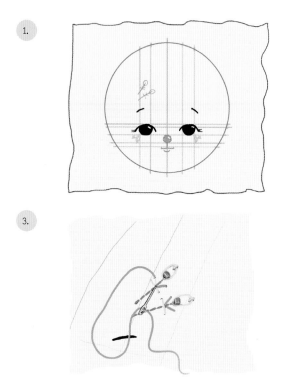

2.

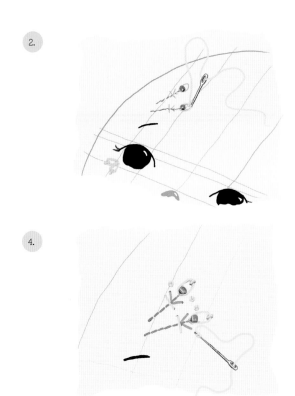

3.

4.

4 Referring to the ear paper pattern piece as a guide, fold each fabric ear over where indicated by the dotted line on the paper pattern piece and pin. To attach the ears to the head, pin each ear onto the marked area at the top of the head using Fig 7 as a guide for placement. Ladder stitch the front and back of each ear onto the head seam.

5 To complete the head and the rest of the body, refer to the Basic Doll chapter.

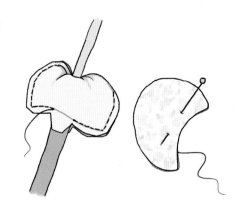

6.

5.

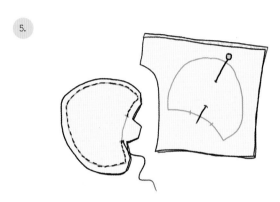

7.

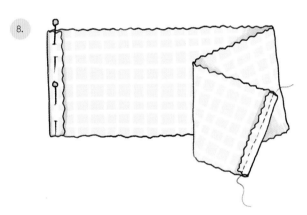

SUMMER TOP

> **YOU WILL NEED**

- 30.5cm x 7cm (12in x 2¾in) lightweight cotton fabric for top skirt
- 20.5cm x 10cm (8in x 4in) lightweight cotton fabric for bodice, to match skirt
- Machine sewing thread to match top fabric
- One 5mm (¼in) snap closure
- Straw and chopstick/orange stick

8.

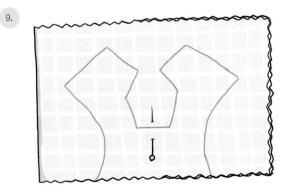

LAYOUT, CUTTING AND SEWING

1 Pin the top skirt pattern piece onto the folded piece of 30.5cm x 7cm (12in x 2¾in) fabric and cut out with pinking shears. Alternatively, cut out the piece with dressmaking scissors and zig-zag around the edges with your sewing machine. Fold in the short sides of the top skirt on both sides of the fabric, wrong sides facing, about 5mm (¼in) and pin (Fig 8). Machine sew the folded edges of the top skirt down either side.

2 For the bodice, fold the 20.5cm x 10cm (8in x 4in) piece of fabric in half widthways, right sides facing. Trace the outline of the bodice directly onto the wrong side of the fabric with a disappearing-ink marker, placing the bottom edge of the bodice onto the bottom edge of the fabric (Fig 9). Pin them together.

9.

3 To sew the top, stitch around each armhole, beginning at the dot marked A on Fig 10 and sewing along the curve to the dot at B, stitching directly onto the marked outline and beginning and ending the seam with a few back stitches. Repeat on the opposite side. Now stitch along the side of the back, beginning at dot C, continuing around the neckline and down the opposite side and ending at dot D (beginning and ending the seam with back stitches). Snip the corners and trim excess fabric around the sewn edges (Fig 11). Turn the bodice right side out, using a straw and chopstick or orange stick to help with turning (Fig 12). Now use the stick to gently push out the corners and then press flat.

4 Pin the bottom and back edges of the bodice front and back together. Machine sew the bottom edges closed with a small zig-zag stitch (Fig 13). Fold the bodice over at the shoulders, matching the zig-zagged edges at the front and back, and then pin (Fig 14). Hand stitch a couple of stitches close to the bottom edge on either side to join the front and back together (Fig 15).

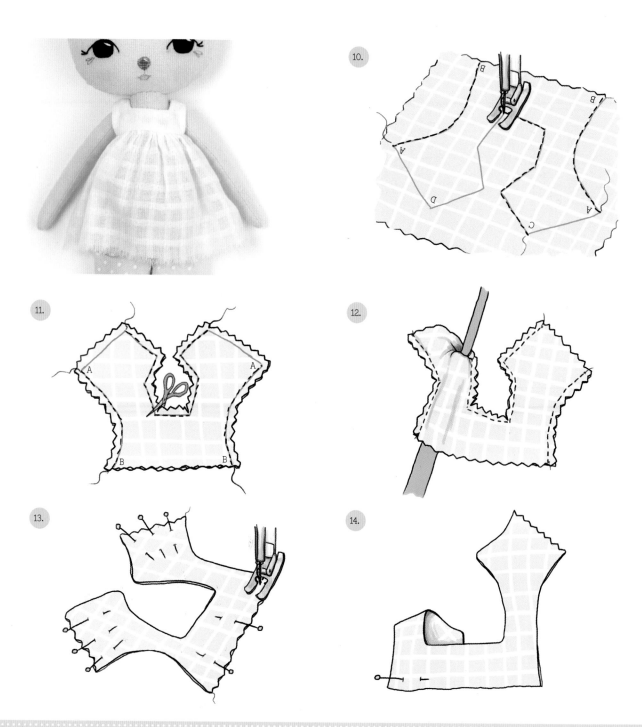

5 To attach the bodice to the skirt, set your machine stitch on the longest stitch setting (gathering stitch) and sew three rows of gathering stitches about 5mm (¼in) below the top edge of the skirt, leaving long threads on either side for pulling up the gathers later (Fig 16). Fold the skirt in half and mark the centre along the top edge on the right side of the fabric with a disappearing-ink marker. Repeat the process and mark the centre line at the bottom edge of the inside of the bodice. Match the centre dot on the bottom edge of the bodice with the centre dot on the top edge of the skirt, right sides facing, and pin at the centre (Fig 17). Pin the left-hand side edge of the bodice to the left-hand side edge of the skirt, and then pin the right-hand side edge of the bodice to the right-hand side edge of the skirt.

6 Gently pull the gathers on either side of the skirt until the width of the skirt matches the width of the bodice, pinning along the top edge (Fig 18). To ensure that the gathers are even, use the back of a large needle to spread them evenly across the top edge of the skirt. Set your machine stitch on a regular stitch and position the fabric on the bed of the machine so that the needle is about 5mm (¼in) away from the edge of the skirt/bodice. Stitch the bodice to the skirt, remove the gathering threads and press the seam up (Fig 19).

7 Fit the top onto the doll and turn it around so that the back of the doll is facing you. Determine where the snap closure should be and mark the area on each side of the bodice with a disappearing-ink marker. Remove the top and sew the snaps in place (Fig 20).

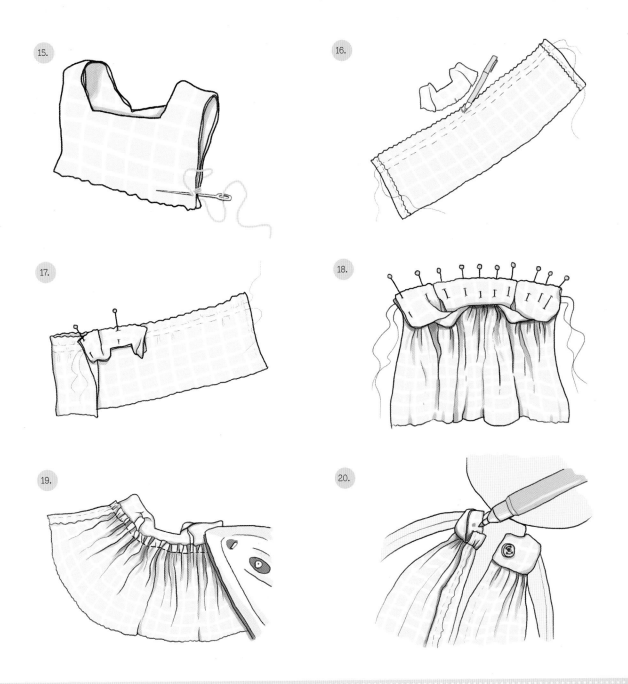

15.

16.

17.

18.

19.

20.

CAPRI PANTS

YOU WILL NEED

- Two pieces 11.5cm x 15cm (4½in x 6in) cotton fabric for capri pants
- Machine sewing thread to match fabric
- DMC Cotton embroidery thread (floss) in pink (3708)

LAYOUT, CUTTING AND SEWING

1 Place the two pieces of fabric together, right sides facing and pin the capri pants paper pattern onto the fabric and cut out. When assembling the capris please note that all seams are machine sewn 5mm (¼in) away from the fabric edges. Beginning on the right-hand side, pin the fabric together from the waistband at the point marked A on Fig 21, following the curve of the crotch to B. Stitch this seam about 5mm (¼in) away from the edge. This will be the front seam of the capris. Open the fabric and press the front seam open. Fold the top edge of the pants over about 5mm (¼in) to create a waistband. Press the top edge down and pin (Fig 22). Fold the bottom of each leg opening up about 5mm (¼in) to create a hem. Press flat and pin.

2 Machine stitch the waistband and hems, sewing about 1mm–2mm (¹/₁₆in–⅛in) away from the cut edge. Fold the pants in half lengthways, right sides facing. Pin the fabric together from the waistband at A (Fig 23), following the curve of the crotch to B, and then stitch the seam about 5mm (¼in) away from the edge, leaving a tail of thread at the top of the seam for neatening the waistband. Flatten the seam and use the tail of machine thread to stitch each side of the seam down onto the waistband, being careful to stitch onto the top layer of the fabric, so your stitches aren't visible from the right side of the fabric.

21.

22.

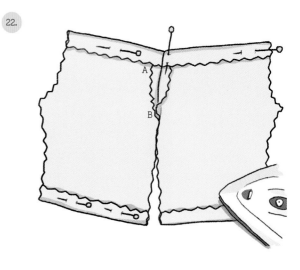

23.

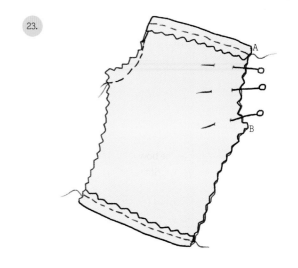

Tip

IF YOU LIKE, YOU CAN ADD A PRETTY TRIM
ALONG THE HEMS OF THE CAPRI PANTS.
PIN THE TRIM ONTO THE FOLDED HEMS
BEFORE MACHINE STITCHING THEM.

3 To sew the inner leg seam, match the dots at the crotch at B, right sides facing and pin along the centre of the seam (Fig 24). Match the bottom edges of each pant leg at the dots marked at C and pin. Sew the inner leg seam from C to C, leaving a tail of thread at the beginning and end of the seam for neatening the leg openings. Use small, sharp scissors to notch around the curve at the crotch, being careful not to snip into your stitched seam. Use the tail of machine thread to neaten the seam edges of the leg openings, in the same way that you neatened the back seam of the waistband.

4 Turn the capris right side out. Thread a needle with three strands of pink embroidery thread about 40.5cm (16in) long. Knot the end. Create a drawstring by sewing small running stitches around the middle of the waistband. Even out the drawstring so that there's an even length on either side of the centre seam. Fit the capris onto the doll and tie the thread into a bow. Snip off excess thread and tie a knot on each end.

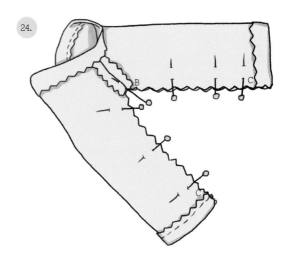

BOW

YOU WILL NEED

- 10cm x 6.5cm (4in x 2½in) felt for bow
- Embroidery thread to match felt
- Button pin 2cm (¾in) for attaching the bow (optional) – see also Tip, below

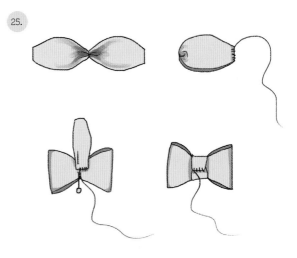

LAYOUT, CUTTING AND SEWING

1 Pin the bow pattern pieces onto the felt and cut out. Follow Fig 25 for the sequence of sewing the bow. Begin by folding the bow in half lengthways, right sides facing and sew a few tight stitches at the centre on the wrong side of the bow to create a permanent pinch. Fold the bow in half widthways and blanket stitch the two short ends together. Fold the bow so that the blanket stitches run down the centre. Position the short edge of the bow centre onto the centre of the blanket stitches and whip stitch the short edge onto the centre of the blanket stitches. Wrap the bow centre around over the front of the bow and overlap the opposite short edge onto the stitched edge. Stitch in place.

2 Attach the button pin onto the centre back of the bow. To finish, pin the bow to the mouse's head, placing it just below the base of an ear.

Tip

USING A BUTTON PIN MEANS THAT THE TOY IS NOT SUITABLE FOR YOUNG CHILDREN FOR SAFETY REASONS. OLDER CHILDREN SHOULD BE SUPERVISED WHEN ATTACHING OR REMOVING THE PIN.

WHIMSICAL MOUSE
PATTERNS

The Mouse also requires the Basic Doll patterns – see end of Basic Doll chapter. All the patterns are actual size, so there is no need to enlarge or reduce them. Printable versions of these patterns can be downloaded from: http://ideas.sewandso.co.uk/patterns.

HEAD
TRACE 1 ONTO FABRIC

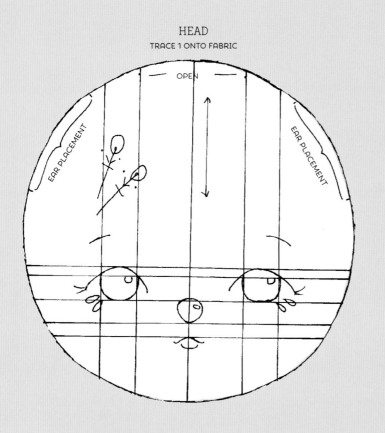

LEFT EAR

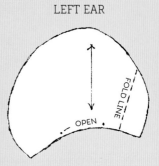

EARS
TRACE 1 OF EACH ONTO
LAYERED FABRICS

RIGHT EAR

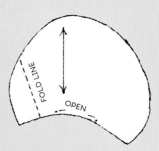

SUMMER TOP
BODICE
TRACE 1 ONTO
FOLDED FABRIC

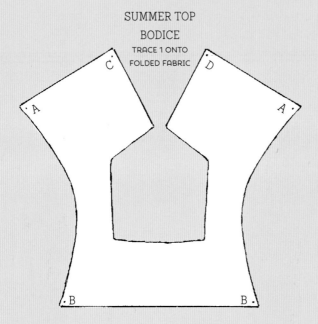

SUMMER TOP SKIRT
CUT 1 ON FOLD

PLACE ON FOLD OF FABRIC

BOW
CUT 1 FROM FELT

BOW CENTRE
CUT 1 FROM FELT

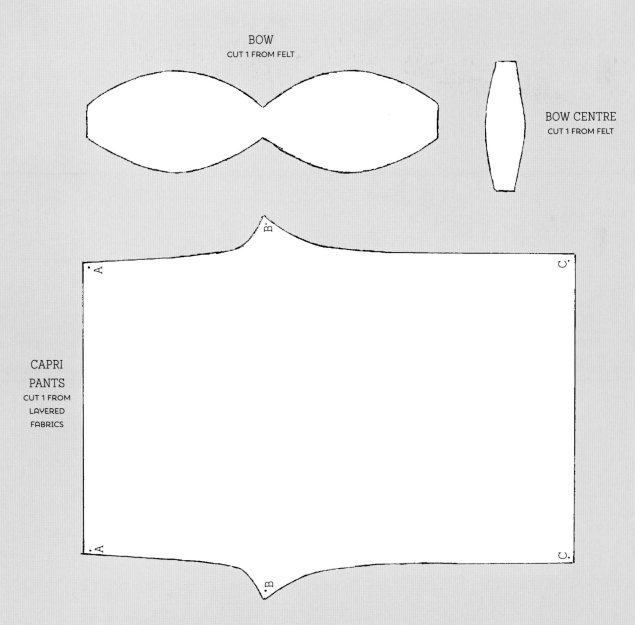

CAPRI
PANTS
CUT 1 FROM
LAYERED
FABRICS

A

B

C

A

B

C

DAPPER
Bear

This dear little bear is dressed in shorts made from a smart striped fabric. Tiny bright pink buttons add a pop of colour to the felt shoulder straps. His look is completed with an easy-to-knit mohair scarf wrapped snugly around his neck. A busy little bee is embroidered on his forehead – perhaps he, too, is dreaming of honey?

YOU WILL NEED

FACE AND BEE EMBROIDERY

- DMC Cotton embroidery thread (floss): black (310) for eyes, eyebrows, bee head and body stripes and pale orange (3854) for bee body stripes
- DMC Satin embroidery thread: white (S5200) for eye and snout highlights
- DMC Light Effects: silver (E168) for bee wings and turquoise (E3849) for dashed line
- Lecien Cosmo Nishikiito Metallic thread: copper (16) for snout (or DMC Light Effects thread copper (E301) for a similar look)
- Embroidery needle
- Disappearing-ink marker, ruler and embroidery hoop

HAND EMBROIDERY STITCHES USED

Refer to the Stitch Guide chapter for these stitches.

- Stem stitch
- Satin stitch
- Straight stitch
- Running stitch
- Ladder stitch

MAKING THE BASIC DOLL

Refer to the Basic Doll chapter to make the doll and transfer the head facial features and embroidery motifs onto the bear's head. Embroider the facial features (eyes and snout) as indicated in the Basic Doll chapter, Embroidering the Facial Features. All embroidery is worked with one strand of thread unless otherwise stated.

WORKING THE HEAD EMBROIDERY MOTIFS

1 To embroider the bee, begin by filling in the head with satin stitch using one strand of black embroidery thread, keeping your stitches close together. Because of its small size, I have not outlined the head in stem stitch. Continuing with the black thread, embroider the antennae with small straight stitches. Fill in the top area of the bee's body with a couple of short straight stitches placed at the neck area and then stitch a couple of longer straight stitches directly below the short stitches for the first stripe, keeping the stitches close together (Fig 1). Now stitch the remaining stripes, using two straight stitches for each stripe. Fill in the stinger with a few short straight stitches. Use pale orange thread to fill in the body between each stripe with small straight stitches, keeping the stitches close together inside the marked lines of the body (Fig 2).

2 To embroider the bee's wings, use one strand of silver Light Effects thread and outline each wing in stem stitch. To complete the bee, use one strand of turquoise Light Effects to stitch the dashed line with running stitch (Fig 3).

3 To complete the head and the rest of the body, refer to the Basic Doll chapter.

1.

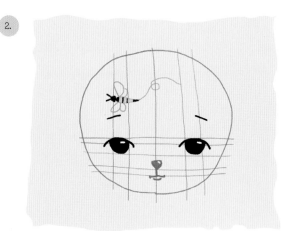

2.

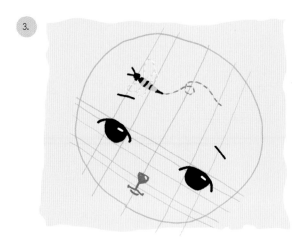

3.

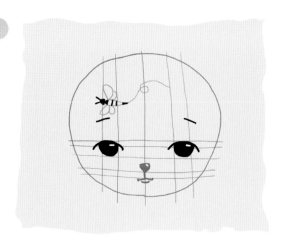

EARS

YOU WILL NEED

- Two pieces 7.5cm x 10cm (3in x 4in) cotton fabric
- Machine sewing thread to match fabric
- Small amount of stuffing (fiber fill)

LAYOUT, CUTTING AND MAKING

1 Place the fabric pieces together, right sides facing. Using a disappearing-ink marker, trace the left and right ear patterns directly onto the fabric, transferring the dots for the opening at the base of the ears. Pin the pieces together (Fig 4). Stitch around each ear, beginning at one dot at the opening of the ear and sewing around to the dot on the opposite side, leaving the area between the dots open for turning and stuffing (Fig 5). Begin and end each seam with a back stitch and leave a long tail of thread at the end, for sewing the openings closed. Trim excess fabric around each ear, leaving a little tab between the dots for the openings. Turn the ears right side out and ladder stitch the openings closed.

2 To attach the ears to the head, pin each ear onto the marked area at the top of the head. Ladder stitch the front and back of each ear onto the head seam (Fig 6).

4.

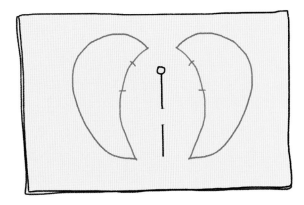

5.

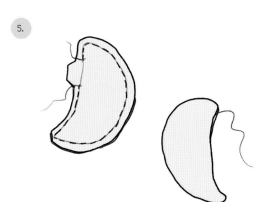

6.

SHORTS

YOU WILL NEED

- Two pieces cotton fabric 12.5cm (5in) square for shorts
- Two pieces felt 1cm x 12.5cm (⅜in x 5in) for straps
- Two tiny 5mm (¼in) buttons
- Machine sewing thread to match shorts fabric
- Embroidery thread, contrasting or matching, for waistband and turn-ups

LAYOUT, CUTTING AND SEWING

1 Pin the paper pattern pieces for the left and right sides of the shorts onto the 12.5cm (5in) pieces of fabric. Cut out the fabric. To transfer the dart markings at the top of each fabric pattern piece, keep the pattern pinned in place, lift the top edge of paper and use a disappearing-ink marker to mark the beginning of the lines onto the fabric. Remove the pattern and use a ruler to continue each marked line onto the fabric, about 2.5cm (1in) down from the top of the waistband. These will help with placement of the darts later.

2 When assembling the shorts, all seams are machine sewn 5mm (¼in) away from fabric edges. Pin the shorts pieces together, right sides facing. Following Fig 7 and beginning on the right-hand side, stitch down from the waistband at A, following the curve of the crotch to B, about 5mm (¼in) away from the edge. Repeat on the left-hand side. Press the seams open. Fold the top edge of the shorts over about 5mm (¼in) to create a waistband. Press the top edge down and pin all the way around. Thread a needle with a doubled embroidery thread. You can use a contrasting colour or two different colours together for fun. Using small running stitches, stitch down the waistband (Fig 8).

3 To sew the inner leg seam, follow Fig 9, matching the dots at the crotch at B, right sides facing and pin along the centre of the seam. Match the bottom edges of each pant leg at the dots marked at C and pin. Sew the inner leg seam from C, up and back down to C. Notch around the curve at the crotch, being careful not to snip into your stitched seam. Before turning the shorts right side out, fold the bottom openings of the legs up about 2cm (¾in). Using one strand of matching machine thread, tack (baste) about 5mm (¼in) away from the fabric's cut edge (Fig 10).

7.

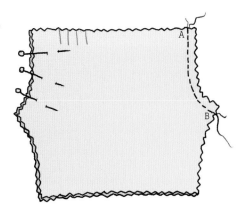

8.

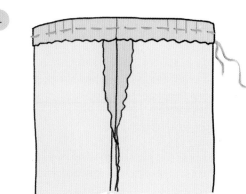

9.

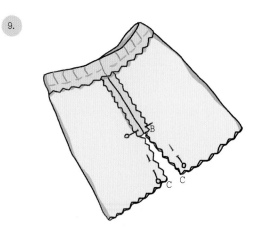

10.

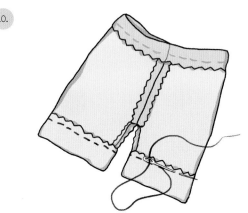

4 To create the waistband darts, turn the shorts right side out and fit them onto the bear. Begin the darts by pinching along the line marked 2 on Fig 11 at the top of the waistband, to create a vertical fold about 2.5cm (1in) long. Now fold the waistband over sideways so the pinched fold along the line marked 2 on Fig 12 aligns with the line marked at 4 below it. Secure the dart in place with a pin and repeat on the opposite side. Remove the shorts from the bear and using one strand of matching machine thread, secure each dart in place with a couple of hand stitches (Fig 13). Remove the pins.

5 To make the straps, use the pattern piece to cut two lengths of felt each 1cm x 12.5cm (⅜in x 5in). Pin the short end of one strap onto the area where you've made the dart on the waistband and secure in place with a couple of tiny hand stitches. Place a tiny button directly on top of the stitches and sew the button onto the strap. Repeat with the other strap.

6 To create the little turn-ups at the bottom of each leg of the shorts, fold the bottom edge of each leg up by about 5mm (¼in) and pin. Thread a needle with a doubled embroidery thread. You can use a contrasting colour or two different colours together. Using hand running stitches, stitch the turn-ups in place.

7 Fit the shorts onto the bear. Place the straps over each shoulder, crossing them at the back. Tuck each end into the waistband at the back, spacing them evenly from the centre seam. Pin in place and then secure with a few cross stitches (Fig 14).

SCARF

YOU WILL NEED

- Three-ply yarn: 1 strand each of Rowan Kidsilk Mohair in lavender and aqua
- Knitting needles size 3mm

KNITTING THE SCARF

Using the two strands of yarn together, cast on 7 stitches. Stocking stitch (stockinette stitch) for 132 rows (knit one row, purl one row). Cast (bind) off. Tie a knot at both ends of the scarf. Loop the scarf in half and wrap it around the bear's neck, threading the ends through the loop and gently pulling until the scarf sits snugly around his neck.

If you prefer, you can create a scarf from felt or jersey fabric by cutting a piece 2cm (¾in) wide x 51cm (20in) long.

11.

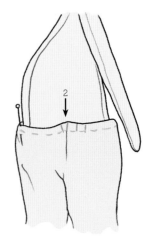

12.

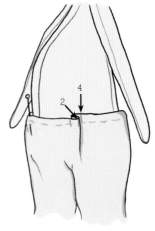

13.

14.

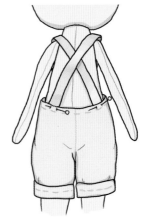

DAPPER BEAR
PATTERNS

The Bear also requires the Basic Doll patterns – see end of Basic Doll chapter. All the patterns are actual size, so there is no need to enlarge or reduce them. Printable versions of these patterns can be downloaded from: http://ideas.sewandso.co.uk/patterns.

HEAD
TRACE 1 ONTO FABRIC

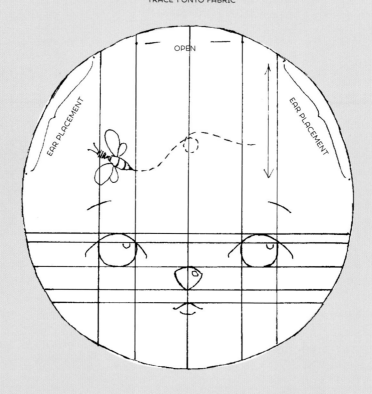

EARS
TRACE 1 OF EACH ONTO
LAYERED FABRICS

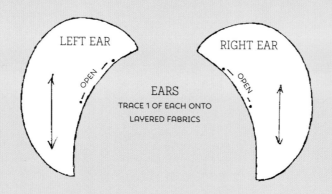

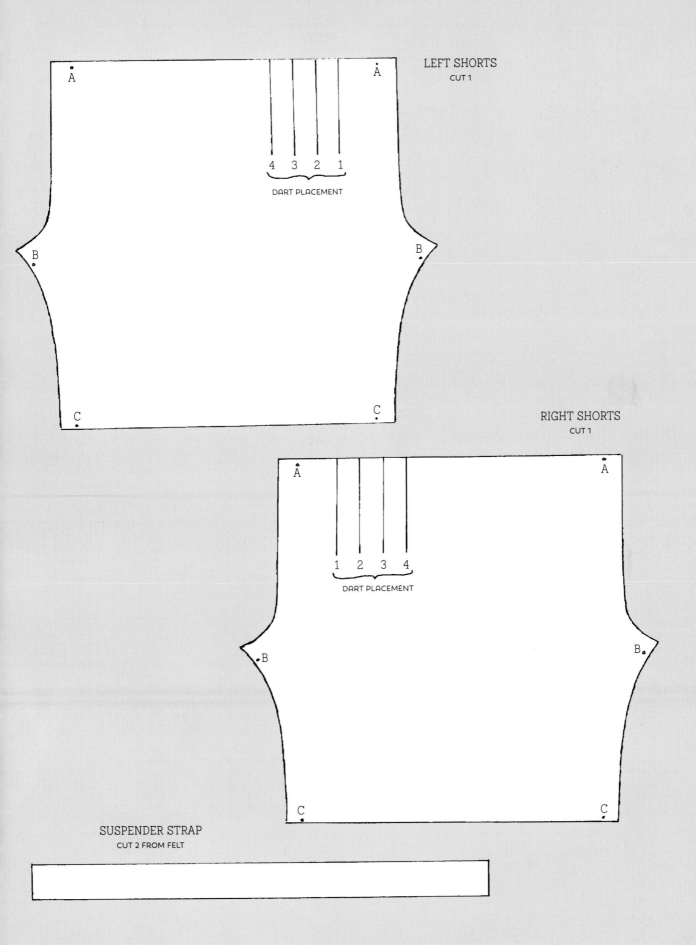

LEFT SHORTS
CUT 1

4 3 2 1

DART PLACEMENT

RIGHT SHORTS
CUT 1

1 2 3 4

DART PLACEMENT

SUSPENDER STRAP
CUT 2 FROM FELT

DREAMY *Owl*

Delicately embroidered features and feathery fabric ears give this little owl a soft and dreamy look. She wears a pretty blush-hued dress made from a lightweight lawn, which is overlaid with a tissue-thin, shimmery gauze fabric.

YOU WILL NEED

FACE AND DECORATIVE EMBROIDERY

- DMC Cotton embroidery thread (floss): black (310) for eyes, pink (3708), yellow (744), lavender (209), turquoise (3849), light orange (402) for feathers, brown (3862) and golden-brown (434) for beak and chartreuse (907) for French knots
- DMC Satin embroidery thread: white (S5200) for eye and beak highlights (or white Cotton embroidery thread)
- Lecien Cosmo Nishikiito Metallic thread: copper (16) for beak (or DMC Light Effects thread copper (E301) for a similar look)
- Embroidery needle
- Disappearing-ink marker, ruler and embroidery hoop

HAND EMBROIDERY STITCHES USED

Refer to the Stitch Guide chapter for these stitches.

- Stem stitch
- Satin stitch
- Straight stitch
- Back stitch
- French knot
- Ladder stitch

MAKING THE BASIC DOLL

Refer to the Basic Doll chapter to make the doll and transfer the facial features and embroidery motifs onto the head.

WORKING THE HEAD EMBROIDERY MOTIFS

1 For the facial embroidery use one strand of thread. Embroider the beak first, outlining it with stem stitch using one strand of copper thread. Fill in the beak with horizontal satin stitches, spacing them about 1mm (¹/₁₆in) apart (Fig 1). Do not end off the thread. Using the same thread and beginning in the centre of the beak, fill in the beak from the centre to one side with vertical satin stitches, spacing them about 1mm (¹/₁₆in) apart (Fig 2). Repeat on the other side. These horizontally and vertically placed stitches create a grid pattern and a slightly raised look. Working separately with the brown and golden-brown threads, fill in the beak with vertical satin stitches (Fig 3), alternating the two colours between the vertical lines of the copper thread (Fig 4).

2 Embroider the owl's eyes as indicated in the Basic Doll chapter and add white highlights in each eye and along the top right-hand side of the beak (Fig 5). For the feathered brows on either side of the eyes, use back stitch and one strand of thread – use turquoise for the smallest feathers at the top, use lavender for the middle ones and pink for the bottom two.

3 Embroider the feathers on the forehead with stem stitches (Fig 6). Begin by stitching the first two feathers in the centre just above the eyes with one strand of turquoise thread, then proceed up to the two outer feathers on the row above, stitching them with pink. Stitch the feathers in the centre of the second row with yellow. For the next row, stitch the outer feathers in turquoise and the inner feathers in lavender. Complete the top feathers using light orange. Stitch French knots onto the dots marked above the feathered brows and within the forehead with one strand of chartreuse, winding the thread around the needle three times to form each knot.

4 To complete the head and the rest of the body, refer to the Basic Doll chapter; make the legs but do not make arms as the owl will have wings instead.

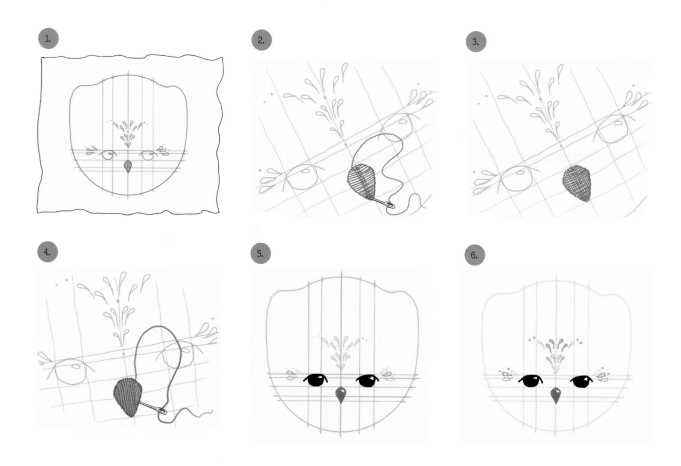

WINGS

- 12.5cm (5in) square cotton fabric for outer wings, to match main body and head
- 12.5cm (5in) square fabric in pink satin or cotton for inner wings
- Machine sewing thread to match main fabric
- Long doll needle

LAYOUT, CUTTING AND SEWING

1 Place the outer wing fabric and inner wing fabric together, right sides facing. Using a disappearing-ink marker, trace both wing patterns directly onto the cotton fabric, transferring the dots for openings along the outer edges of each wing (Fig 7). Pin the pieces together. Stitch around each wing, beginning at one dot and sewing around to the dot on the opposite side, leaving the area between the dots open for turning. Begin and end each seam with a back stitch and leave a long tail of thread for sewing the openings closed. Trim excess fabric around each wing, leaving a little tab between the dots for the openings.

2 Turn the wings right side out, using a chopstick or orange stick to round out the shoulder area and the curves along the bottom of each wing (Fig 8). Tuck the tabs in and ladder stitch the openings closed. Press the wings firmly so they lay very flat.

3 To attach the wings to the body, pin them to the sides of the body. Using a double-threaded long doll needle (I like to use embroidery thread), insert the needle underneath one wing and take it through the body and out through the wing on the opposite side (Fig 9). Bring the needle through the same wing again, back through the body and out through the other wing. Go back and forth a few times and end off under a wing.

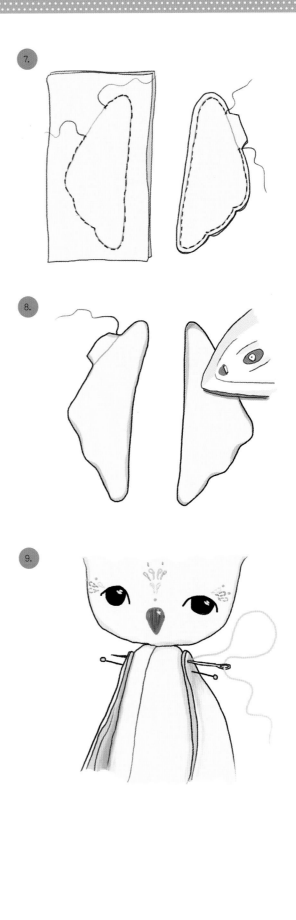

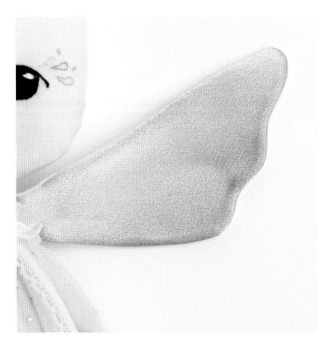

EAR FEATHERS

- 7.5cm x 10cm (3in x 4in) pink linen or cotton fabric
- Cotton embroidery thread (floss) to match fabric

LAYOUT, CUTTING AND SEWING

1 Trace the outlines of the left and right ear feathers onto the fabric using a fabric marker. Marking the numbers on each one as indicated on the pattern pieces will help with placement (Fig 10).

2 To create each feathered ear, stack the wider, rounded ends of the left-hand side feathers on top of each other, beginning with the largest piece marked 1, then adding the second one marked 2 and lastly, the smallest one marked 3. Do the same with the right-hand side feathers (Fig 11). Now gently fan the feathers out, keeping the wider ends overlapped to prevent them from separating. Hand stitch the wider ends of the stack together about 3mm (⅛in) from the edges using one strand of embroidery thread, making sure to stitch through all the pieces. Keep the thread uncut, for attaching to the head later.

3 To attach the ear feathers, pin the base of each feather bundle onto the area marked for the ears on the top of the head, fanning the feathers out and over the ear nubs on either side of the head (Fig 12). Use the tail of thread to sew the feathers into place, keeping the stitches small and neat and hidden beneath the feathered bundles.

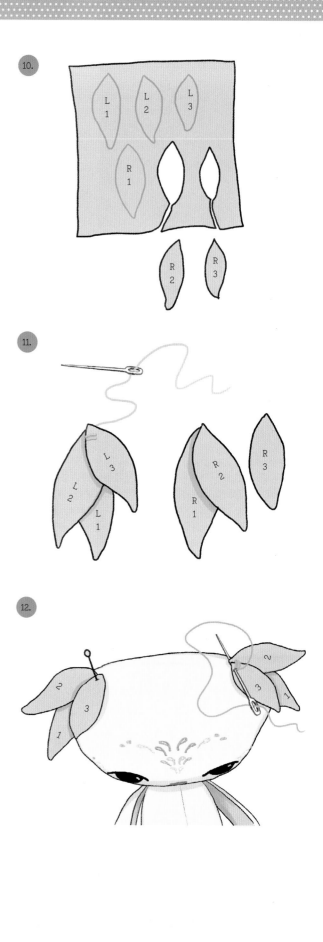

DRESS

YOU WILL NEED

- 35.5cm x 15cm (14in x 6in) lightweight cotton fabric for dress
- 29cm x 14cm (11½in x 5½in) glitter netting for skirt overlay
- Machine sewing thread to match dress fabric
- 1.5cm x 28cm (½in x 11in) trim for hem
- One 5mm (¼in) snap closure
- 2cm (¾in) wide silk bow or flower for accent
- Two pieces of ribbon and/or lace each 3mm x 15cm (⅛in x 6in), for accent
- One seed bead for accent
- Orange stick or chopstick
- Fray Check or fabric glue

LAYOUT, CUTTING AND SEWING

1 Pin the dress skirt pattern piece onto the folded lightweight cotton fabric and cut out with pinking shears. Alternatively, cut out the pieces with dressmaking scissors and zig-zag around the edges with your sewing machine. Pin the skirt overlay pattern piece onto the folded piece of netting and cut out with pinking shears.

2 For the dress bodice, fold the remaining dress skirt fabric in half lengthways, right sides facing, and trace the outline of the bodice directly onto the wrong side of the fabric with a disappearing-ink marker, and then pin together (Fig 13).

3 To sew the dress, start by stitching around the top and sides of the dress bodice, sewing directly onto the marked outline (Fig 14). Trim excess fabric around the sewn edge and along the bottom edge of the bodice. Fold in the short sides of the dress skirt on either side of the fabric about 5mm (¼in), wrong sides facing, and pin. Machine sew the folded edges of the dress skirt down on either side.

4 Turn the bodice right side out, using a chopstick/orange stick to gently push out the corners. Press flat and pin the bottom edges together. Machine sew the bottom edges closed with a small zig-zag stitch. With a disappearing-ink marker, mark the centre line at the bottom edge of the bodice on the wrong side of the fabric (Fig 15). Fold up a 5mm (¼in) hem along the bottom of the dress skirt. Pin and tack (baste) the hem in place.

5 Measure the bottom edge of the skirt, cutting your trim to match. Run a small bead of Fray Check or fabric glue onto the cut edges and allow to dry thoroughly. Pin the trim onto the wrong side of the fabric and machine stitch in place (Fig 16). Remove the tacking (basting).

13.

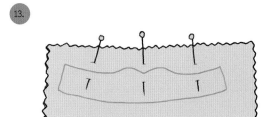

14.

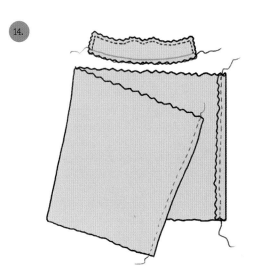

15.

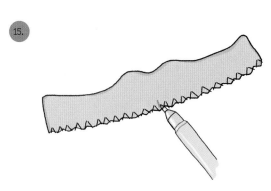

16.

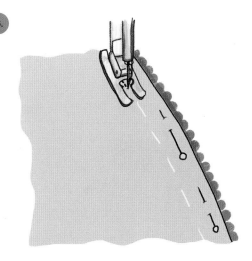

6 Pin the top long edge of the netting onto the top edge of the fabric skirt (Fig 17). Neaten off any excess fabric from the sides with pinking shears. Set the machine stitch on the longest stitch setting (gathering stitch) and sew three rows of gathering stitches about 5mm (¼in) below the top edge of the skirt, leaving long threads on either side for pulling up the gathers later (Fig 18). Fold the skirt in half and mark the centre along the top edge on the right side of the fabric with a disappearing-ink marker (Fig 19).

7 To attach the bodice to the dress skirt, match the centre dot on the bottom edge of the bodice with the centre dot on the top edge of the skirt, right sides facing, and pin at the centre. Pin the side edges of the skirt to the side edges of the bodice, and then gently begin pulling the threads on one side. Notice that there are six gathering threads on either side of the skirt. To ensure that your gathers are even, only pull the top layer of threads from either side. Gently pull the gathers on either side of the skirt until the width of the skirt matches the width of the bodice. To ensure that your gathers are even, use the back of a needle to spread them evenly across the top edge. Fig 20 shows what the work should look like from the reverse, and Fig 21 shows what the work should look like from the front, once gathered. Set your machine on a regular stitch length and position the fabric so that the needle is about 5mm (¼in) away from the edge of the skirt/bodice edge. Stitch the bodice to the skirt (Fig 22). Remove the gathering threads, pressing the seam upwards.

8 Fit the dress onto the doll and turn it so that the back of the doll is facing you. Determine where the snap closure should be and mark the area on each side of the bodice with a disappearing-ink marker (Fig 23). Remove the dress and sew the snaps in place.

9 To attach the decorative accent onto the front of the dress, fit the dress onto the doll and pin the bow/flower onto the bodice seam, placing it just off-centre (Fig 24). To mark the placement, slide the bow/flower up the stem of the pin and use a fabric marker to mark the spot at the base of the pin (Fig 25).

10 Lay one lace/ribbon onto the second one, matching the short edges, and stitch the ends together (Fig 26). Don't end off the thread. Position the bow/flower onto the stitched area of the ribbons and stitch in place with a couple of stitches, keeping the thread attached (Fig 27). Remove the dress from the doll and sew the bow onto the spot marked at the front of the dress, adding a tiny seed bead to the centre if desired (Fig 28).

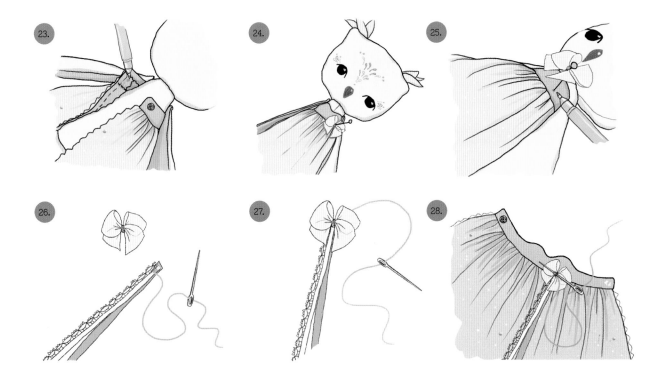

DREAMY OWL PATTERNS

The Owl also requires the Basic Doll patterns – see end of Basic Doll chapter. All the patterns are actual size, so there is no need to enlarge or reduce them. Printable versions of these patterns can be downloaded from: http://ideas.sewandso.co.uk/patterns.

HEAD
TRACE 1 ONTO
FABRIC

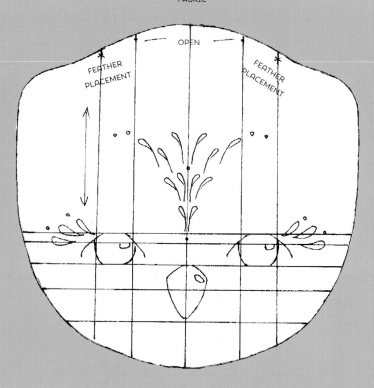

OPEN

FEATHER PLACEMENT

FEATHER PLACEMENT

DRESS BODICE
TRACE 1 ONTO
FOLDED FABRIC

DRESS SKIRT OVERLAY

CUT 1 ON FOLD

PLACE ON FOLD OF FABRIC

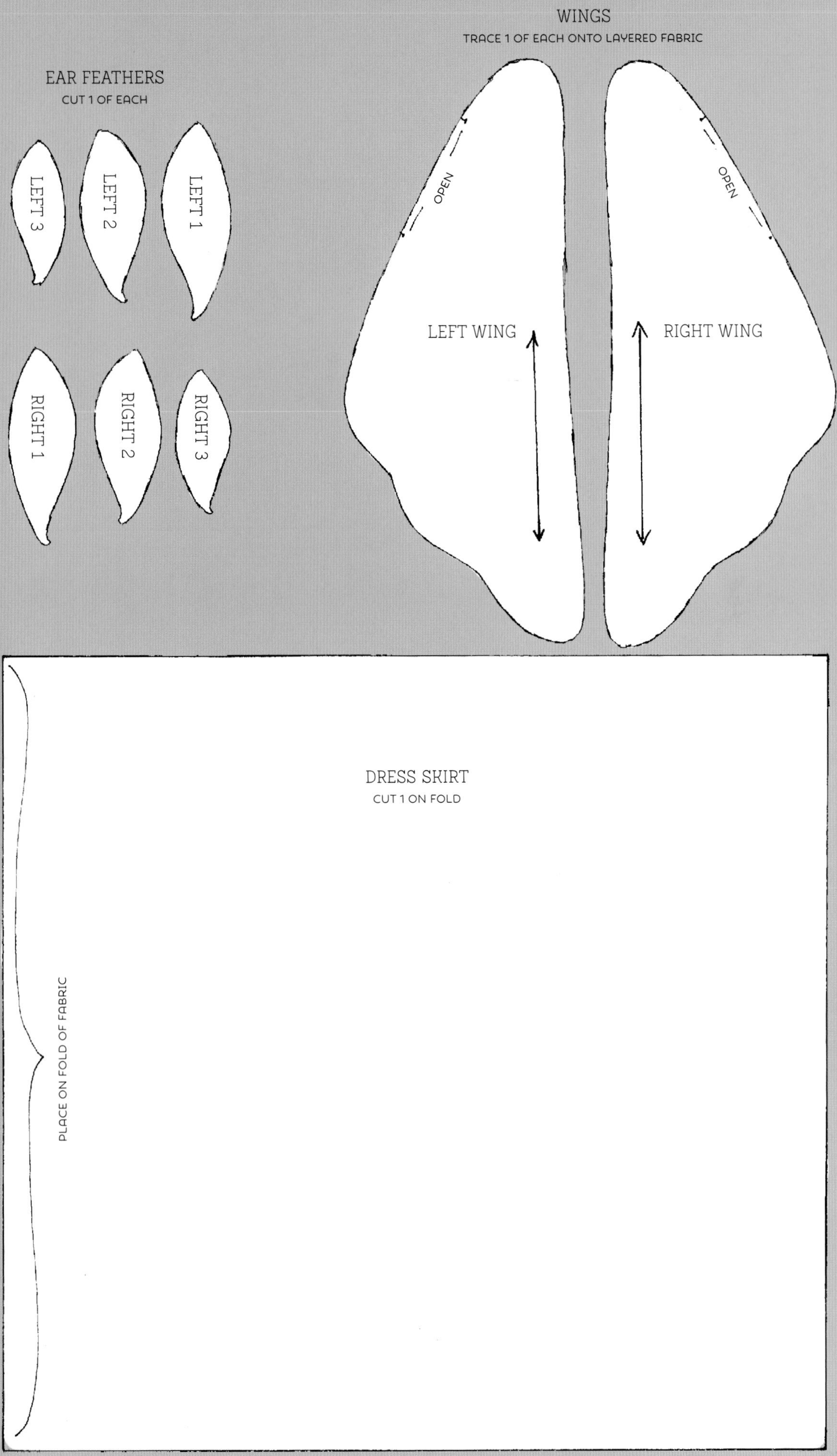

EAR FEATHERS
CUT 1 OF EACH

LEFT 3

LEFT 2

LEFT 1

RIGHT 1

RIGHT 2

RIGHT 3

WINGS
TRACE 1 OF EACH ONTO LAYERED FABRIC

OPEN

OPEN

LEFT WING

RIGHT WING

DRESS SKIRT
CUT 1 ON FOLD

PLACE ON FOLD OF FABRIC

DARLING
Ellie

This darling little budding ballerina is dressed in a fluffy pink tutu made from dozens of tulle strips looped around a simple ribbon waistband. A pretty corset top, adorned with dazzling crystals, sparkles in the light, while delicate ribbons wrapped around her legs add a finishing touch.

YOU WILL NEED

FACE AND FLORAL EMBROIDERY

- DMC Cotton embroidery thread (floss): black (310) for eyes and eyebrows, medium pink (3716), light pink (761), yellow (744) and light orange (402) for lazy daisy flowers, aqua (964) for French knots, moss green (3012) for leaves
- DMC Satin embroidery thread: white (S5200) for eye and snout highlights (or white Cotton embroidery thread)
- DMC Color Variations embroidery thread: pink (4180) for roses
- Embroidery needle and large-eyed embroidery needle
- Disappearing-ink marker, ruler and embroidery hoop

HAND EMBROIDERY STITCHES USED

Refer to the Stitch Guide chapter for these stitches.

- Stem stitch
- Satin stitch
- Straight stitch
- Lazy daisy stitch
- Woven wheel stitch
- French knot
- Ladder stitch
- Whip stitch

MAKING THE BASIC DOLL

Refer to the Basic Doll chapter to make the doll and transfer the head facial features and embroidery motifs onto the doll's head. Embroider the facial features (eyes, eyelashes and eyebrows) as indicated in the Basic Doll chapter, Embroidering the Facial Features.

WORKING THE HEAD EMBROIDERY MOTIFS

1 The roses are stitched with four strands of embroidery thread, and the petal flowers and leaves with one strand. To make the roses, thread a large-eyed embroidery needle with four strands of pink DMC Color Variations thread and follow the directions in the Stitch Guide for making the woven wheel stitch in the centre of one of the roses. Repeat the process for the remaining roses (Fig 1).

2 To stitch the flowers and leaves, embroider each one with lazy daisy stitches, using medium pink, light pink, yellow and light orange for the flowers and moss green for the leaves (Fig 2). Stitch French knots onto the dots with one strand of aqua thread. Wind the thread around the needle three times before inserting it into the fabric to form the knot (Fig 3).

3 To complete the head and the rest of the body, refer to the Basic Doll chapter.

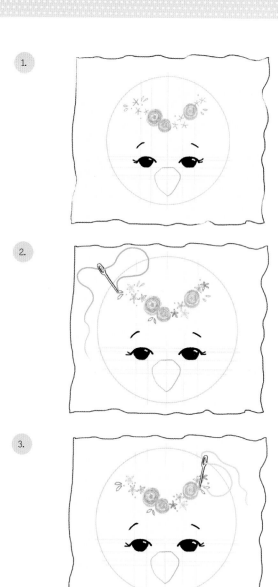

EARS AND TRUNK

YOU WILL NEED

- 18cm x 28cm (7in x 11in) cotton fabric in contrasting colour
- Embroidery thread to match trunk fabric
- Stuffing (fiber fill) for trunk
- Cotton bud (Q-tip)

LAYOUT, CUTTING AND SEWING

1 Fold the fabric in half widthways, right sides facing. Using a disappearing-ink marker, trace the trunk and left and right ear patterns directly onto the fabric, transferring dots for the openings along the sides of each piece. Mark the gathering lines on the trunk. Pin the pieces together (Fig 4).

2 Stitch around each piece, beginning at one dot and sewing around to the dot on the opposite side of the opening, leaving the area between the dots open for turning and stuffing (Fig 5). Begin and end each seam with a back stitch and leave a long tail of thread once you've reached the dot on the opposite side for sewing the openings closed. Trim excess fabric around the trunk and each ear, leaving a little tab between the dots for the openings. Notch curves along the bottom edge of the trunk, being careful not to snip into the stitches.

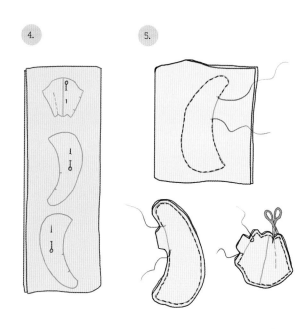

3 Turn the ears and trunk right side out and press flat. Using the trunk pattern piece as a guide, transfer markings for gathering lines onto the trunk (Fig 6). Double thread a needle with embroidery thread to match the trunk colour and run a line of tiny gathering stitches along the marked line, hiding the knot inside the trunk. Do not end off the thread. Fold the trunk along each of the marked lines and pin. Whip stitch the sides of the trunk together beginning at the wider end and ending at the narrow end and leaving a tail of thread attached (Fig 7). Insert a cotton bud (Q-tip) into the trunk and push it firmly into the small opening at the narrow end. Now fold the tip over and whip stitch the tiny opening closed (Fig 8).

4 To attach the ears and trunk to the head, pin each ear onto the marked area along the side of the head, folding the top curve of each ear over as shown in Fig 9. Ladder stitch the front and back of each ear onto the head seam. Stuff the trunk fairly firmly. Pin the trunk onto the area marked below the eyes (Fig 10). Ladder stitch the trunk onto the face, going around a couple of times to secure it (Fig 11). Now gently pull the gathering threads to create a little curve at the tip of the trunk (Fig 12). When happy with how it looks, secure the thread and end off.

BALLET TOP

YOU WILL NEED

- 18cm x 20.5cm (7in x 8in) cotton fabric
- Machine sewing thread to match fabric
- Six 2mm ($^1/_{16}$in) flat-backed Swarovski crystals
- Three 5mm (¼in) snap closures
- Clear-drying craft glue, cotton buds (Q-tips) and a pair of tweezers or fine pliers

LAYOUT, CUTTING AND SEWING

1 Fold the fabric for the ballet top in half widthways, right sides facing. Trace the top pattern onto the fabric with a disappearing-ink marker, transferring the dots for the opening along the side. Pin the pieces together. Sew directly onto the marked line between the dots, beginning and ending the seam with a back stitch and leaving a long tail of thread for sewing up the opening later. Trim excess fabric around the edges, leaving a little tab between the dots for the opening along the side of the top (Fig 13). Notch around curves, being careful not to cut into the stitches. Turn the top right side out and tuck the tab in along the seam. Pin the edges together, ladder stitch the opening closed and press.

2 Using the top pattern piece as a guide, transfer the pattern markings for the crystals onto the front (Fig 14). Use tweezers or fine pliers to pick up a crystal, dip the pointed end of a cotton bud (Q-tip) into glue and dab it onto the back of the crystal. Position the crystal onto a marked dot, pushing it down firmly (Fig 15). Repeat with the remaining crystals and allow all to dry thoroughly.

3 Place the top onto the doll, mark the spots for the snap closures along the back sides and then stitch them in place (Fig 16).

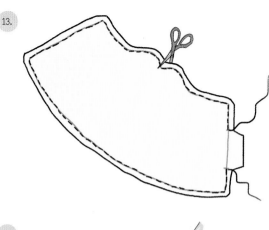

13.

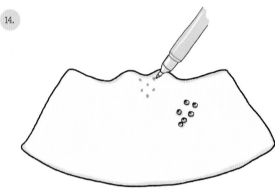

14.

15.

16.

TUTU AND CROSS-OVER LACES

YOU WILL NEED

- Five pieces of tulle, each 46cm x 12.5cm (18in x 5in)
- Ribbon or seam binding 1.5cm x 33cm (½in x 13in)
- Clips or pins
- Two pieces of ribbon each 3mm x 51cm (⅛in x 20in) long, for laces

LAYOUT, CUTTING AND SEWING

1 To prepare the tulle strips, fold one strip in half lengthways and clip or pin the cut edges together (Fig 17). Fold the strip in half widthways, repositioning the clips along the top edge. Cut the tulle in half widthways along the fold (Fig 18). Now fold the strip in half widthways once more, again repositioning the clips along the cut edge. Cut the folded edges running down the sides of the strip.

2 You should now have a sandwiched pile of tulle measuring about 11.5cm (4½in) across the widest part of the pile. Place pins/clips along the bottom edge to ensure that the pile does not slip when you attempt to cut the smaller strips. Using a tape measure and a disappearing-ink marker, divide the strip into three equal sections, as follows (Fig 19). Place the tape measure along the top edge of the strip, aligning the edge of the tape measure with the left-hand edge of the strip. Use your marker to mark a dot at 4cm (1½in), and then mark a second dot 4cm (1½in) away from the first dot. Repeat the process along the bottom edge of the strip, and then mark lines to connect the dots with a ruler. Cut along the marked lines and remove the pins. You should end up with twelve strips 4cm x 12.5cm (1½in x 5in). Repeat the process for the remaining four 46cm x 12.5cm (18in x 5in) tulle strips. This will give you a total of sixty strips.

3 To attach the tulle strips to the ribbon waistband, mark the centre of the ribbon/seam binding with a disappearing-ink marker. Place the ribbon around the doll's waist tying it in a bow behind her back. Mark the areas on either side of the bow with your marker and remove from the waist. The tulle strips will be attached onto the area between these two dots.

17.

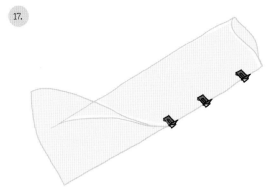

18.

19.

Tip

PRETTY GLASS BEADS CAN BE
USED INSTEAD OF THE SWAROVSKI
CRYSTALS; JUST STITCH THEM
ONTO THE MARKED DOTS.

4 To attach each strip of tulle onto the waistband, fold a strip of tulle in half lengthways to form a loop. Place the middle of the loop behind the waistband ribbon, placing it near the centre of the ribbon. Position it so that there's about 2.5cm (1in) of the loop showing from behind the ribbon. Now flip the two bottom edges of the strip up and over the front of the ribbon and into the loop. Gently pull the strips so that they're even on both sides, then slide the looped area onto the dot marked at the centre of the ribbon, securing it snugly as you do so by pulling both strips at the same time. Do not pull too tightly (Fig 20). Work your way around the waistband in this manner until you reach the dot on the opposite end. Now begin again at the centre and work your way around to the other side, sliding the strips together closely to create a full and fluffy tutu. You can cut more strips if necessary. Trim along the bottom of the tulle to neaten any uneven edges (Fig 21). Fit the tutu onto the doll, making a bow at the back.

5 To make the laces, wrap the ribbons around the lower part of the legs, crossing them over twice and then tying in a bow on the outside of the leg (Fig 22).

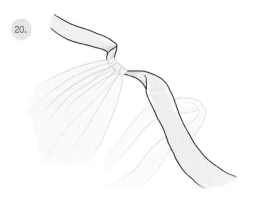

20.

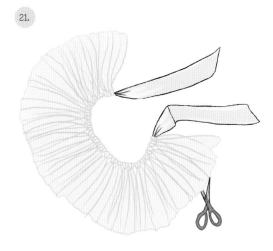

21.

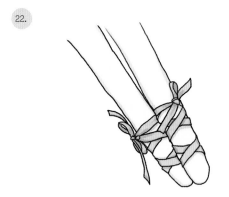

22.

DARLING ELLIE
PATTERNS

The Elephant also requires the Basic Doll patterns – see end of Basic Doll chapter. All the patterns are actual size, so there is no need to enlarge or reduce them. Printable versions of these patterns can be downloaded from: http://ideas.sewandso.co.uk/patterns.

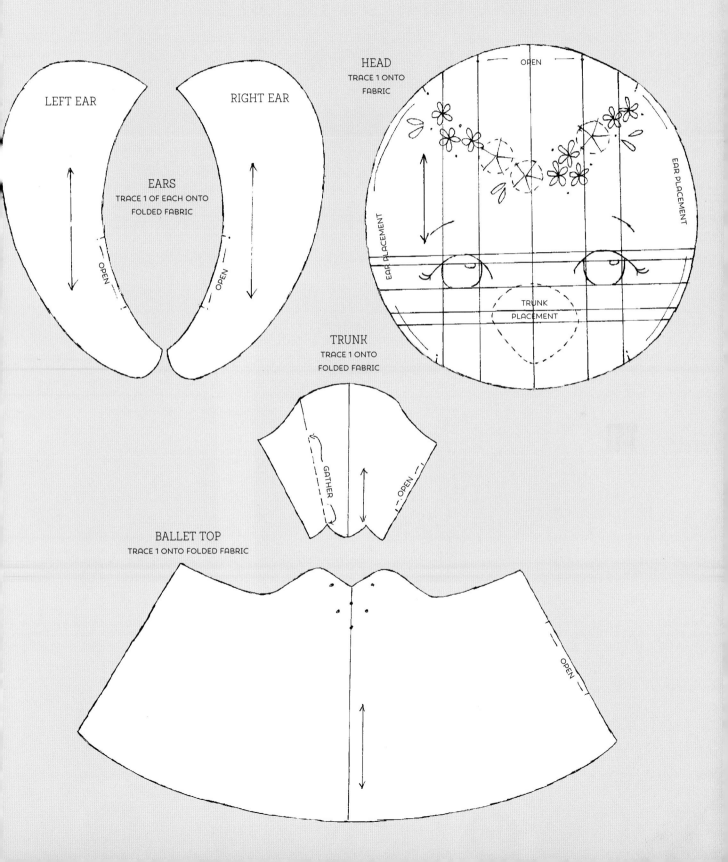

LEFT EAR

RIGHT EAR

EARS
TRACE 1 OF EACH ONTO
FOLDED FABRIC

OPEN

OPEN

HEAD
TRACE 1 ONTO
FABRIC

OPEN

EAR PLACEMENT

EAR PLACEMENT

TRUNK
PLACEMENT

TRUNK
TRACE 1 ONTO
FOLDED FABRIC

GATHER

OPEN

BALLET TOP
TRACE 1 ONTO FOLDED FABRIC

OPEN

NAUTICAL
Fox

Ahoy there! Are you ready to go sailing? This charming fellow loves to race his sailboat across the pond with his pals. His crisp white top is accented with an embroidered sailboat in navy blue and he wears knickerbockers edged with a tiny pompom trim. To top off his look, a mint green neckerchief is knotted jauntily around his neck.

FACE AND BEADED EMBROIDERY

- DMC Cotton embroidery thread (floss): black (310) for eyes and eyebrows
- DMC Satin embroidery thread: white (S5200) for eye and snout highlights (or white Cotton embroidery thread)
- DMC Light Effects embroidery thread: blue topaz (E334) for adding beads
- Lecien Cosmo Nishikiito Metallic thread: red (14) and copper (16) for snout (or DMC Light Effects thread E815 and E301 for a similar look)
- Twenty-two 5mm (¼in) straight tube beads in navy blue or similar colour
- Embroidery needle and beading needle
- Disappearing-ink marker, ruler and embroidery hoop

HAND EMBROIDERY STITCHES USED

Refer to the Stitch Guide chapter for these stitches.

- Stem stitch
- Satin stitch
- Straight stitch
- Back stitch
- Running stitch
- Ladder stitch

MAKING THE BASIC DOLL

Refer to the Basic Doll chapter to make the doll and transfer the head facial features and embroidery motifs onto the doll's head. Embroider the facial features (eyes and snout) as indicated in the Basic Doll chapter, Embroidering the Facial Features. All facial embroidery is done with one strand of thread unless otherwise stated. The outline for the snout is embroidered with red metallic thread, then filled in with a slightly wider spaced satin stitch. Switch to the copper metallic thread and fill in the open spaces so that you end up with a two-toned look.

WORKING THE HEAD EMBROIDERY MOTIFS

1 The marked lines on the fox's forehead are a guide for the tube bead placement. To attach the beads onto the head, insert a beading needle threaded with the blue Light Effects thread up through the base of the first line marked at the centre of the forehead (just above the eyes). Thread a bead onto the needle, slide the bead down onto the fabric and then insert the tip of the needle into the fabric at the opposite end of the bead to secure it in place. Repeat this process twice so that you have secured the bead with two strands of thread (Fig 1). Continue stitching the beads onto the marked lines on the forehead in this manner, working upwards from row to row (Fig 2).

2 To complete the head and the rest of the body, refer to the Basic Doll chapter.

1.

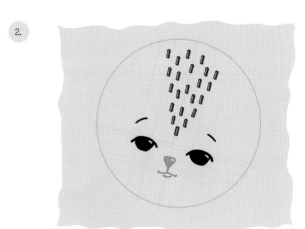

2.

INSTEAD OF USING STRAIGHT BEADS ON YOUR FOX'S FOREHEAD AND EARS, YOU COULD DOUBLE THREAD A NEEDLE WITH SPARKLY EMBROIDERY THREAD AND USE STRAIGHT STITCHES ON EACH AREA.

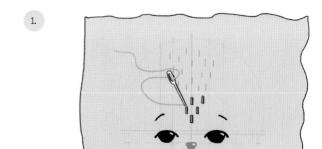

EARS

YOU WILL
NEED

- 6.5cm x 11.5cm (2½in x 4½in) cotton fabric for outer ears, to match body and head
- 6.5cm x 11.5cm (2½in x 4½in) fabric in white for inner ears
- Machine sewing thread to match main fabric
- Six 5mm (¼in) straight tube beads in navy blue or similar colour

LAYOUT, CUTTING AND SEWING

1 Place the outer ear fabric and inner ear fabric together, right sides facing. Using a disappearing-ink marker, trace the left and right ear patterns directly onto the fabric, transferring the dots for the opening at the base of the ears. Pin the pieces together.

2 Stitch around each ear, beginning at one dot at the base of the ear and sewing around to the dot on the opposite side, leaving the area between the dots open for turning (Fig 3). Begin and end each seam with a back stitch and leave a long tail of thread once you've reached the dot on the opposite side. Trim excess fabric around each ear, leaving a little tab between the dots for the openings. Turn the ears right side out, tuck the tabs in and ladder stitch the openings closed, leaving a tail of thread for attaching the ears to the head later. Press the work. Using the ear paper pattern pieces as a guide, transfer the line markings for the beads at the top of each ear onto the inner ears (white fabric) with a disappearing-ink marker.

3 To attach the three beads onto each of the inner ear tips, use the same thread and the same method as you did when attaching the beads to the forehead, being careful not to stitch through to the fabric on the outer ears (Fig 4).

4 Using the ear paper pattern pieces as a guide, transfer the dotted line for the fold placement onto each inner ear (white fabric) with a disappearing-ink marker. Fold each ear over along the dotted line and pin in place (Fig 5). To attach the ears to the head, pin each ear onto the marked area at the top of the head using Fig 6 to guide with ear placement. Ladder stitch the front and back of each ear onto the head seam (Fig 7).

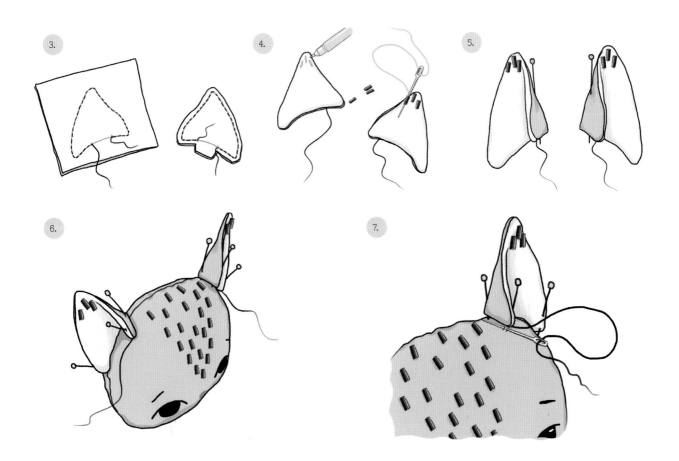

SAILOR SHORTS

YOU WILL NEED

- 12.5cm x 20.5cm (5in x 8in) cotton fabric for shorts
- 1.5cm (½in) wide pompom trim in contrasting colour for leg openings
- Machine sewing thread to match shorts fabric
- Fray Check or fabric glue

LAYOUT, CUTTING AND SEWING

1 Pin the shorts paper pattern piece onto the fabric and cut out. To transfer dart markings and seam markings onto the fabric, keep the paper pattern piece pinned in place and lift the top and side edges of the pattern, and use a disappearing-ink marker to mark the beginning of the lines onto the fabric (Fig 8). Remove the paper pattern and use a ruler to connect the lines running from A to B on either side and the line running down the centre of the fabric, from the centre line at the top of the waistband to D. Now use the ruler to mark the dart lines on either side of the centre line, continuing each line about 3cm (1¼in) from the top of the waistband. These lines will help with the placement of the darts later.

2 To create the darts at the waistband, begin on the right-hand side of the centre line and pinch along the marked line at the point marked 1, to create a vertical fold about 5cm (2in) long (Fig 9). Fold the pinched line over towards the centre line at D and pin the dart in place. Repeat the process on the left-hand side of the centre line, pinning the dart in place on the other side. Double thread a needle with machine thread and back stitch the darts in place, stitching about 3mm (⅛in) below the top edge of the shorts and stitching across the top of the darted area (Fig 10).

3 Fold the top edge of the shorts over to the wrong side about 5mm (¼in) to create a waistband. Press the top edge down and pin. Machine stitch the waistband, sewing about 1mm–2mm (¹/₁₆in) away from the cut edge of the fabric.

4 Fold the bottom of each leg opening up about 5mm (¼in) to create a hem. Press flat and pin (Fig 11). Cut trim to match the length of the hems and apply a small bead of Fray Check or fabric glue to the cut ends of the trim and allow to dry thoroughly. Tack (baste) the hems in place. Pin the trim onto the hem from the wrong side of the shorts and machine stitch in place (Fig 12). Remove the tacking (basting) stitches.

5 To assemble the shorts, sew the back seam, folding the shorts in half, right sides of fabric facing, matching the dots at A and B and pin. Stitch from A to B, sewing about 5mm (¼in) away from the fabric edge, leaving a tail of thread at the beginning of the seam for neatening the waistband seam (Fig 13). To neaten the top edges of the back seam, flatten the seam and use the left-over machine thread to hand stitch each side down onto the waistband, being careful to stitch onto the top layer of the fabric so that your stitches aren't visible from the right side of the fabric.

6 To sew the inner leg seam, match dots at the crotch at D (Fig 14), right sides facing and pin along the centre of the seam. Match the bottom edges of each pant leg at dots C and pin. Sew the inner leg seam from C to C, leaving a tail of thread at the beginning and end of the seam for neatening the leg openings.

7 Use the tail of machine thread to neaten the seam edges of the leg openings, following the process used to neaten the back seam of the waistband (Fig 15). Notch around the curve at the crotch, being careful not to snip into your stitched seam.

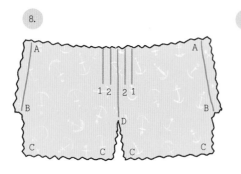

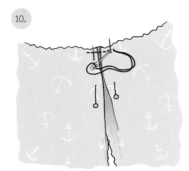

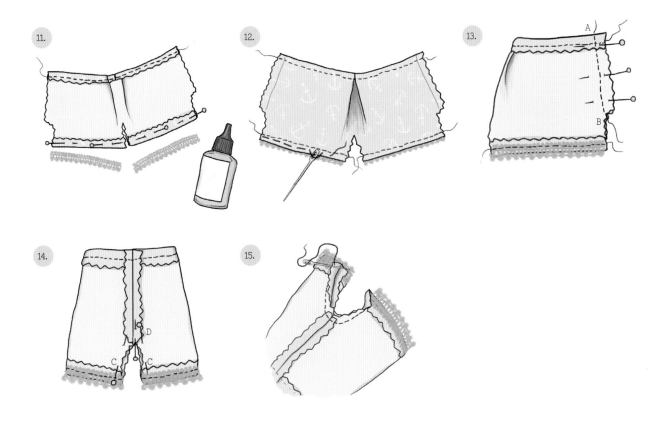

NECKERCHIEF

- 18cm (7in) square lightweight cotton, gauze or knit fabric

LAYOUT, CUTTING AND SEWING

Pin the neckerchief pattern piece onto the fabric, placing the longest side of the triangle on the bias of the fabric, and cut out. With the wrong side of fabric facing up and beginning at the widest end of the triangle, fold the fabric over by 1.5cm (½in) (Fig 16). Continue folding the fabric over until you reach the point at the other end. Place the neckerchief around the fox's neck and tie a jaunty knot at the side.

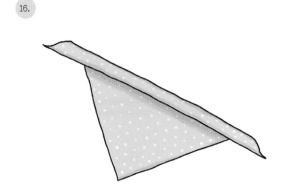

SHIRT

- 20.5cm (8in) square lightweight cotton fabric in white
- Machine sewing thread to match shirt fabric
- DMC Light Effects embroidery thread in dark blue (E825)
- DMC Cotton embroidery thread (floss) in white
- Fray Check or fabric glue

LAYOUT, CUTTING AND SEWING

1 Fold the shirt fabric in half, with the straight grain of the fabric running vertically. Place the shirt pattern piece onto the fold, pin in place and cut out. Open the fabric and with right side facing up, place the fabric onto the paper pattern piece, so that the right-hand side of the shirt matches the outline of the paper pattern below it.

2 To embroider the sailboat, use a disappearing-ink marker to trace the outline of the boat onto the fabric, as well as the marking on the back of the shirt for the opening (Fig 17). Back stitch the boat onto the shirt front using one strand of dark blue Light Effects thread.

3 When assembling the shirt please note that all seams are machine sewn 5mm (¼in) away from the fabric edges. Begin and end all seams with a back stitch. Turn the shirt over so that the wrong side of the fabric is facing up. Fold the sleeve edges over by 5mm (¼in), pin and machine stitch the edges down (Fig 18). Now fold the fabric over so that the front and back side edges match, right sides facing. Pin along the arm and down the side (Fig 19). Repeat on the opposite side. Machine sew around the arms and down the sides, about 5mm (¼in) away from the cut edges of the fabric, leaving a tail of thread at the openings of each arm seam (Fig 20). Snip curves around the armholes. Open the seams and press flat.

4 To neaten the opening of the sleeves, flatten the seam at each arm opening and use the tail of machine thread to stitch each side of the seam down onto the hems, being careful to stitch onto the top layer of the fabric so that your stitches aren't visible from the right side of the fabric (Fig 21). Fold up a 5mm (¼in) hem along the bottom of the shirt (wrong side of fabric) and pin in place (Fig 22). Machine sew the hem.

5 Fold the shirt in half so that the two back sides are aligned, right sides facing. Pin the fabric together below the marked line for the shirt opening (Fig 23). Beginning at the marked line, stitch down to the bottom of the shirt, leaving long tails of thread on either end of the seam. Press the back seam open and use the tail of thread at the bottom of the seam to sew the seam edges onto the hem.

17.
18.
19.
20.
21.

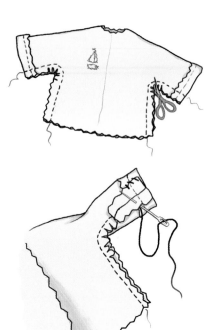

6 For the neck opening, fold the fabric over on either side of the opening at the back of the shirt, so that it matches the pressed seam stitched below the marked line. Press and pin flat (Fig 24). Hand stitch each side down using tiny running stitches (Fig 25). End the thread off at the top on the wrong side of the fabric.

7 Run a small bead of Fray Check or fabric glue along the neckline and allow to dry thoroughly. This will prevent the fabric from fraying and also create a bit of stiffness around the neckline, which will make it easier for you to fold over a tiny hem around the neckline. Once the area is completely dry, fold over a tiny hem about 2mm ($1/16$in) and pin in place (Fig 26). Using white embroidery thread (shown in a dark colour for clarity on Fig 27), hand stitch the neckline using a tiny running stitch. Press the shirt to finish.

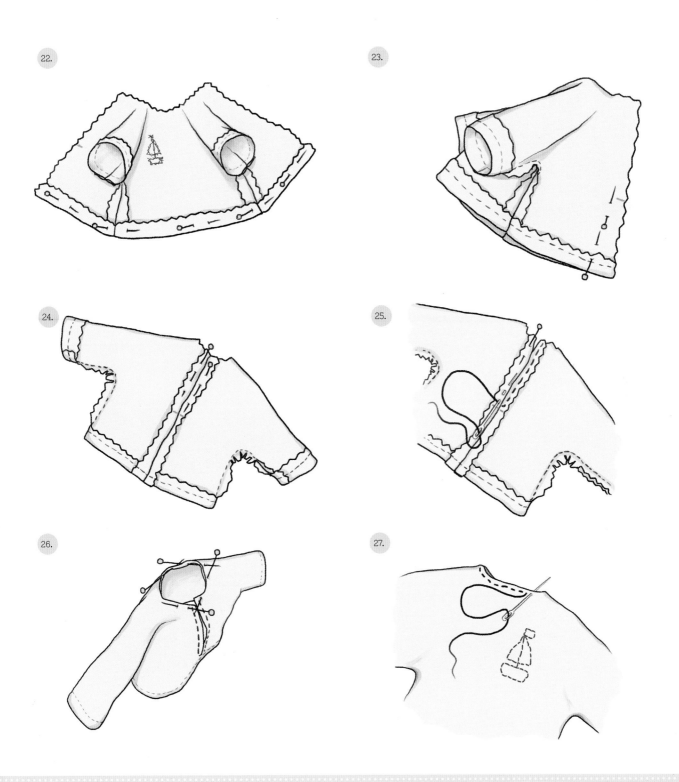

NAUTICAL FOX
PATTERNS

The Fox also requires the Basic Doll patterns – see end of Basic Doll chapter. All the patterns are actual size, so there is no need to enlarge or reduce them. Printable versions of these patterns can be downloaded from: http://ideas.sewandso.co.uk/patterns.

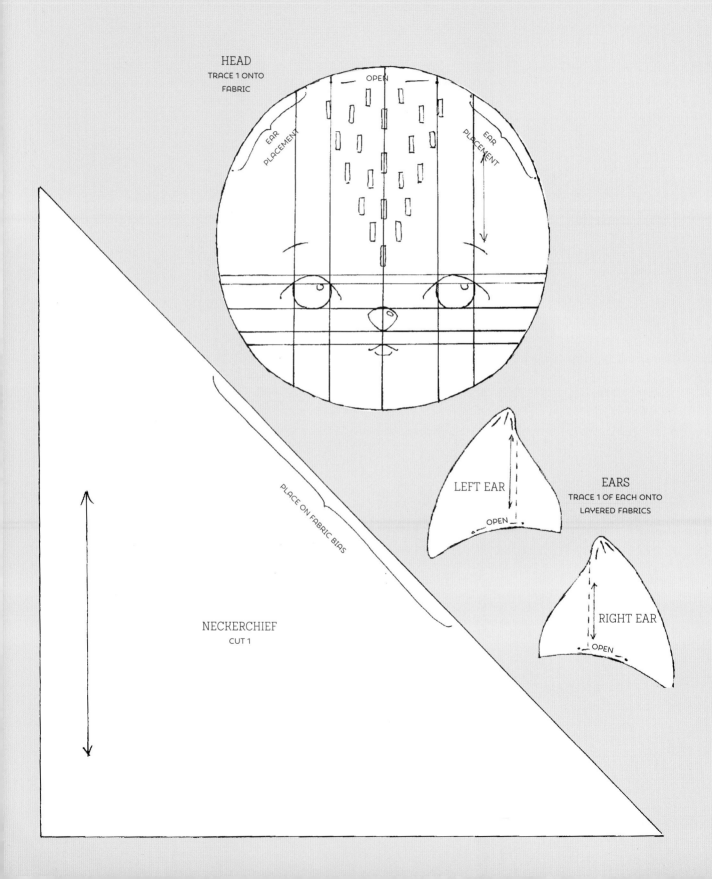

HEAD
TRACE 1 ONTO
FABRIC

OPEN

EAR PLACEMENT

EAR PLACEMENT

PLACE ON FABRIC BIAS

LEFT EAR

OPEN

EARS
TRACE 1 OF EACH ONTO
LAYERED FABRICS

RIGHT EAR

OPEN

NECKERCHIEF
CUT 1

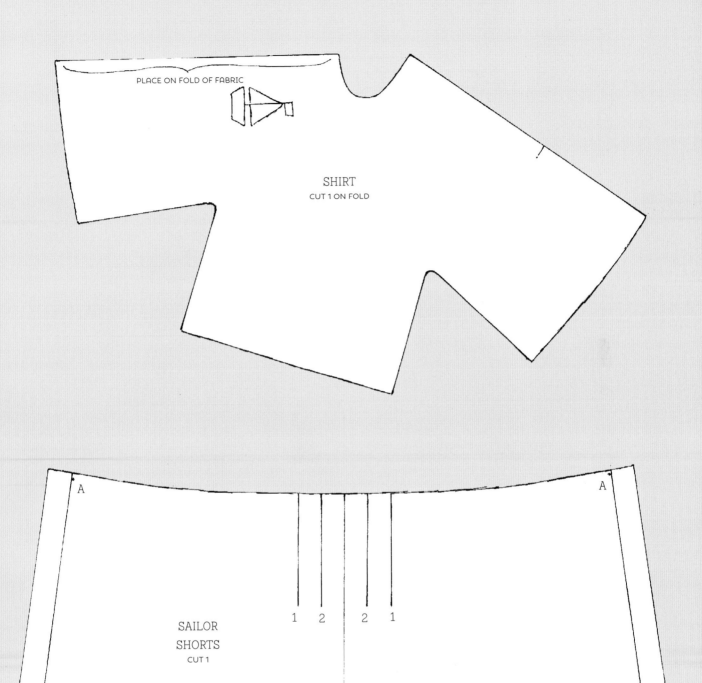

PLACE ON FOLD OF FABRIC

SHIRT
CUT 1 ON FOLD

SAILOR
SHORTS
CUT 1

1   2   2   1

A   A

B   B

C   C

C   C

D

ENCHANTED
Deer

This sweet deer is gorgeously dressed for an enchanted evening out under a moonlit sky. Her pretty dress, made in a dreamy light blue cotton print is complemented by a glamorous faux fur cape tied with a ribbon bow. A decorative spray of embroidered flower and leaves on her forehead is perfect as a tiara.

YOU WILL NEED

FACE AND FLORAL EMBROIDERY

- DMC Cotton embroidery thread (floss): black (310) for eyes and eyebrows, turquoise (3849) for French knots, moss green (3012) for stems and leaves, dark pink (760) and light pink (761) for flower, light yellow (745) and yellow (744) for flower centres and French knots
- DMC Satin embroidery thread: white (S5200) for eye and snout highlights
- Lecien Cosmo Nishikiito Metallic thread: copper (16) for snout (or DMC Light Effects in copper (E301) for a similar look)
- Embroidery needle
- Disappearing-ink marker, ruler and embroidery hoop

HAND EMBROIDERY STITCHES USED

Refer to the Stitch Guide chapter for these stitches.

- Stem stitch
- Satin stitch
- Straight stitch
- Lazy daisy stitch
- French knot
- Ladder stitch
- Whip stitch

MAKING THE BASIC DOLL

Refer to the Basic Doll chapter to make the doll and transfer the head facial features and embroidery motifs onto the deer's head. Embroider the facial features (eyes, eyelashes and snout) as indicated in the Basic Doll chapter, Embroidering the Facial Features. The facial features are embroidered with one strand of embroidery thread and the floral motif is stitched with a combination of one and two strands.

WORKING THE HEAD EMBROIDERY MOTIFS

1 To embroider the floral design, begin by stitching the centre flower in lazy daisy stitch using one strand of light pink and one strand of dark pink together (Fig 1). Outline the stems in stem stitch using one strand of moss green. Embroider the leaves with lazy daisy stitch using one strand of moss green (Fig 2).

2 Using two strands of turquoise thread, stitch French knots onto the dots marked at the outer edges at the top of the stems and leaves. Wind the thread around the needle three times before inserting it into the fabric to form the knot (Fig 3). Using one strand of light yellow and one strand of yellow thread together, stitch French knots onto the dots marked at the base of the stems.

3 To fill in the centre of each flower petal, use one strand of light yellow and one strand of yellow thread together and make a straight stitch (Fig 4).

4 To complete the head and the rest of the body, refer to the Basic Doll chapter.

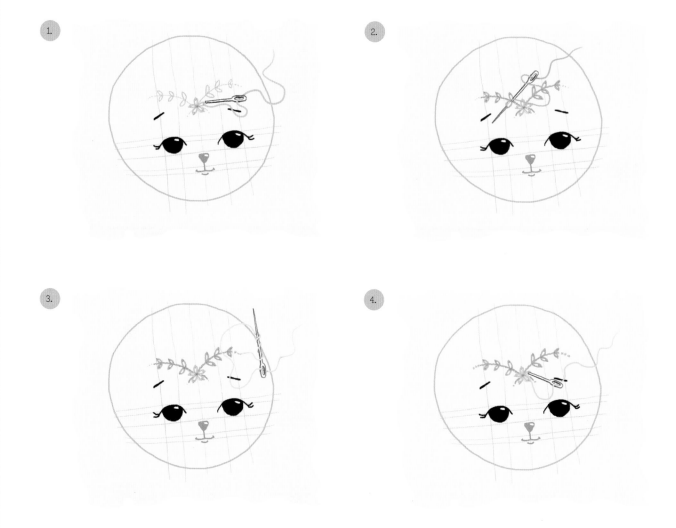

EARS

YOU WILL NEED

- 7.5cm x 10cm (3in x 4in) cotton fabric for outer ears, to match main body and head
- 7.5cm x 10cm (3in x 4in) pink flannel or cotton for inner ears
- Machine sewing thread to match outer ear fabric

LAYOUT, CUTTING AND SEWING

1 Place the outer ear fabric and inner ear fabric together, right sides facing. Using a disappearing-ink marker, trace the left and right ear patterns onto the cotton fabric, transferring the dots for the opening at the base of the ears. Pin the pieces together (Fig 5). Stitch around each ear, beginning at one dot at the base of the ear and sewing around to the dot on the opposite side, leaving the area between the dots open for turning. Begin and end each seam with a back stitch and leave a long tail of thread at the end for sewing the openings closed. Trim excess fabric around each ear, leaving a little tab between the dots.

2 Turn the ears right side out, tuck the tabs in, ladder stitch the openings closed and press. There is no need to stuff. Referring to the ear pattern piece as a guide, fold each fabric ear over where indicated by the dotted line on the pattern and pin. Hand sew the bottom of the ears together with small whip stitches, leaving a tail of thread for attaching the ears to the head later (Fig 6).

3 Attach the ears to the head by pinning each ear onto the marked area at the top of the head (Fig 7). Ladder stitch the front and back of each ear onto the head seam.

5.

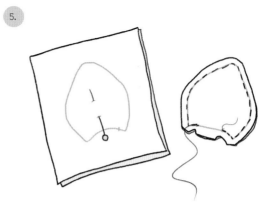

6.

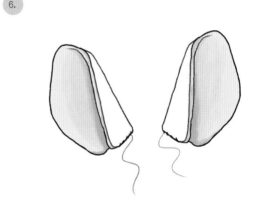

7.

DRESS

- 18cm x 43cm (7in x 17in) lightweight cotton fabric
- Machine sewing thread to match dress fabric
- One 5mm (¼in) snap closure
- Orange stick

LAYOUT, CUTTING AND SEWING

1 Fold the 18cm x 43cm (7in x 17in) piece of cotton in half right sides together and place the left-hand side of the dress skirt pattern on the fabric fold. Mark and then cut out with pinking shears. Alternatively, cut out with dressmaking scissors and zig-zag around the edges with your sewing machine. For the dress bodice, fold the remaining fabric in half widthways, right sides facing and trace the outline of the bodice onto the wrong side of the fabric with a disappearing-ink marker. Pin together (Fig 8). Fold the short sides of the dress skirt over about 5mm (¼in) on either side, wrong sides facing and pin along the folded edges.

2 To sew the dress, stitch around the sides and top of the dress bodice only (do not stitch along the bottom edge), sewing directly onto the marked outline. Trim excess fabric around the sewn edge and along the bottom edge of the bodice (Fig 9). Turn the bodice right side out, using an orange stick to gently push out the corners. Press the bodice flat and pin the bottom edges together. Machine sew the folded edges of the dress skirt down on either side.

3 Machine sew the bottom edge of the bodice closed with a small zig-zag stitch. Fold the bodice in half and use a disappearing-ink marker to mark the centre at the bottom edge of the bodice (Fig 10). Set the machine stitch on the longest stitch setting (gathering stitch) and sew two rows of gathering stitches about 5mm (¼in) below the top edge of the skirt, leaving long threads on either side for pulling up the gathers later. Fold the skirt in half and mark the centre along the top edge on the *right* side of the fabric with a disappearing-ink marker.

4 To attach the bodice to the dress skirt, match the centre dot on the bottom edge of the bodice with the centre dot on the top edge of the skirt, *right* sides facing and pin at the centre. Pin the left-hand side edge of the bodice to the left-hand side edge of the skirt, and then pin the right-hand side edge of the bodice to the right-hand side edge of the skirt. Gently pull the gathers on either side of the skirt until the width of the skirt matches the width of the bodice. Pin along the top edge (Fig 11). To ensure that the gathers are even, use the back of a large needle to spread the gathers evenly across the top edge of the skirt.

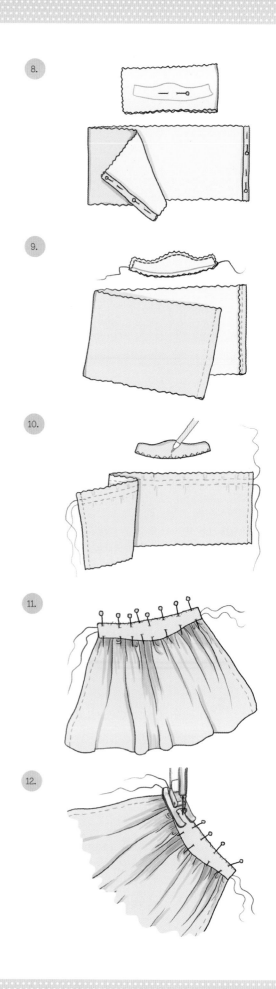

8.

9.

10.

11.

12.

5 Set the machine stitch on a regular stitch and position the fabric so the needle is about 5mm (¼in) away from the top edge of the skirt/bodice edge. Stitch the bodice to the skirt (Fig 12). Remove the gathering threads and press the seam up. Fit the dress onto the doll and turn it around so that the back of the doll is facing you. Determine where the snap closures should be and mark the area on each side of the bodice with a disappearing-ink marker. Remove the dress and sew snaps in place (Fig 13).

6 To complete the dress, you could turn up a small hem along the skirt's bottom edge and stitch it in place by hand or machine. Alternatively, you can leave a raw edge as I have done, using the tip of a fine sewing needle to gently separate and remove a few rows of threads along the bottom edge of the fabric. This will create a slightly frayed, soft raw edge, which is quite pretty.

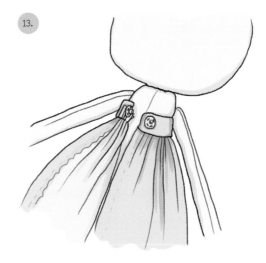

13.

CAPE

YOU WILL NEED

- 10cm x 15cm (4in x 6in) faux fur fabric
- Two pieces of narrow ribbon each 18cm (7in) long
- Fray Check or fabric glue
- Long-nosed embroidery scissors
- Embroidery thread to match ribbon

LAYOUT, CUTTING AND SEWING

1 Please take note of the little arrows marked on the faux fur cape pattern piece – these show in which direction the fur pile should be laying. Trace the cape pattern piece onto the back of the faux fur fabric with a disappearing-ink marker, positioning the arrows in the same direction as the fur pile (Fig 14).

14.

2 Use a sharp pair of long-nosed embroidery scissors to cut out the cape, making sure to *only* cut through the fabric backing (Fig 15). Keep the nose of the scissors underneath the fur pile to prevent you from cutting into the fur. Run a small bead of Fray Check all the way around the cut edge and allow to dry thoroughly. This will help prevent fraying.

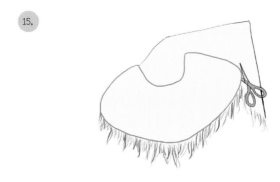

15.

3 Make a knot at each end of the two lengths of narrow ribbon. Position one knotted end onto the top corner on the back of the cape and hand stitch in place with matching embroidery thread. Repeat on the other side (Fig 16). Place the cape around the deer's shoulders and tie a bow at the front.

16.

ENCHANTED DEER
PATTERNS

The Deer also requires the Basic Doll patterns – see end of Basic Doll chapter. All the patterns are actual size, so there is no need to enlarge or reduce them. Printable versions of these patterns can be downloaded from: http://ideas.sewandso.co.uk/patterns.

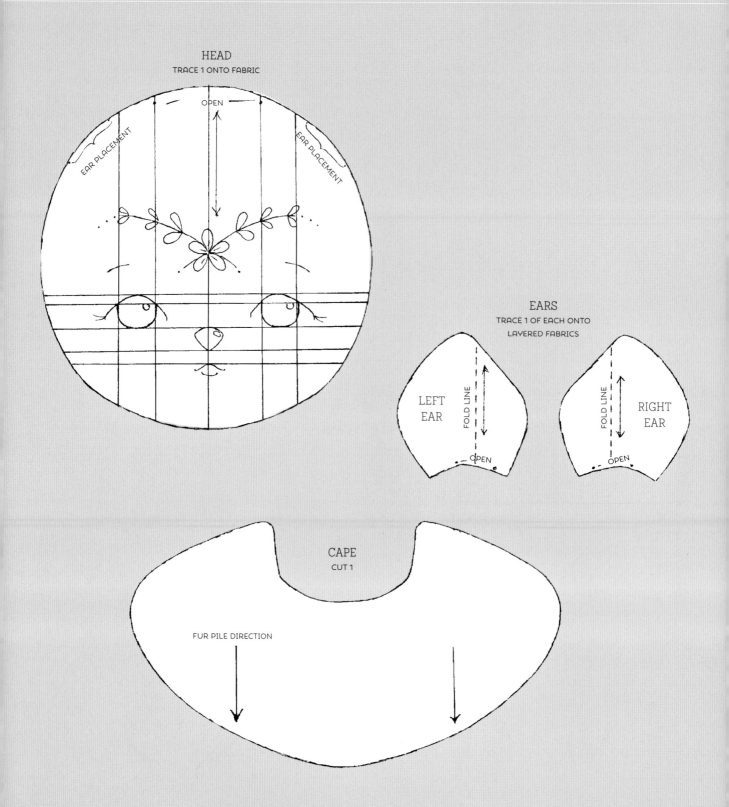

HEAD
TRACE 1 ONTO FABRIC

OPEN

EAR PLACEMENT

EAR PLACEMENT

EARS
TRACE 1 OF EACH ONTO
LAYERED FABRICS

LEFT
EAR

FOLD LINE

OPEN

FOLD LINE

RIGHT
EAR

OPEN

CAPE
CUT 1

FUR PILE DIRECTION

DRESS BODICE

TRACE 1 ONTO

FOLDED FABRIC

DRESS SKIRT

CUT 1 ON FOLD

PLACE ON FOLD OF FABRIC

LULLABY
Lamb

Oh so soft and such a snuggle bun to cuddle with, this adorable little lamb is all ready for bed and dressed in the sweetest pair of floral pyjamas edged in lace! A sprinkling of shimmery embroidered stars frames her features, and a cute bear sleep mask made from felt and stitched by hand, is perfect for completing her outfit.

YOU WILL NEED

FACE AND STAR EMBROIDERY AND FOREHEAD PATCH

- DMC Cotton embroidery thread (floss): black (310) for eyes, dark pink (760) for snout, pink (3708), dark lavender (209) and turquoise (3849) for star, ecru for attaching fur to forehead (or to match fabric)
- DMC Satin embroidery thread: white (S5200) for eye and snout highlights (or white Cotton embroidery thread)
- DMC Light Effects thread: peach (E967) for snout
- 18cm (7in) square cream teddy fur fabric for forehead and body (alternatively, mohair fabric, velour or similar, or a contrasting/patterned cotton fabric in a similar weight to main doll)
- Fray Check or fabric glue if using cotton fabric for forehead (optional)
- Small, sharp embroidery scissors
- Embroidery needle
- Disappearing-ink marker, ruler and embroidery hoop

HAND EMBROIDERY STITCHES USED

Refer to the Stitch Guide chapter for these stitches.

- Stem stitch
- Satin stitch
- Straight stitch
- Back stitch
- Ladder stitch
- Running stitch
- Blanket stitch
- Whip stitch

MAKING THE BASIC DOLL

Refer to the Basic Doll chapter to make the doll and transfer the head facial features and embroidery motifs onto the doll's head. Embroider the facial features (eyes, eyelashes and snout) as indicated in the Basic Doll chapter, Embroidering the Facial Features. For the snout use one strand each of Light Effects peach (E967) and embroidery Cotton in dark pink (760) together in the needle.

WORKING THE HEAD EMBROIDERY MOTIFS

To embroider a star, use one strand of pink, dark lavender or turquoise thread. On one of the stars, insert the needle up from the back of the fabric and out at point A, down at B and up at C (see Fig 1). Take the needle down at point B, come up at D and then down at E (Fig 2). Insert the needle up from the back of the fabric and out at A and down at E. Come up at D and down at C. Fasten off at the back of the fabric (Fig 3). Repeat this process to embroider the other stars using a different colour for each. Don't remove the head fabric from the hoop yet.

1.

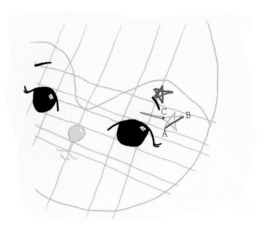

2.

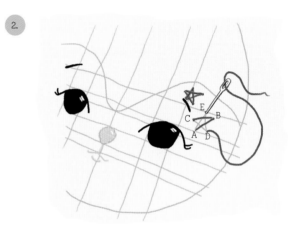

3.

MAKING THE FOREHEAD PATCH

1 Trace the forehead patch pattern piece onto the back of the teddy fur fabric (it looks like knit fabric) with a disappearing-ink marker. Use a small, sharp pair of embroidery scissors to cut out the fur, making sure to cut through the back of the fabric only (Fig 4). Keep the nose of the scissors beneath the fur to prevent cutting into the fur. If you are using an alternative fabric, run a bead of Fray Check or fabric glue along the cut edges of the fabric to prevent fraying.

2 Position the forehead patch onto the head, aligning the curved edge of the fabric with the curved edge marked on the forehead. Secure in place with pins (Fig 5). The top and side edges of the fabric should overlap the marked curve of the top of the head. Working from the *wrong* side of the fabric and beginning at the dot marked A on Fig 6, stitch the curved edge of the forehead patch onto the head using one strand of matching embroidery thread (ecru if using teddy fur fabric). Use a small running stitch and place stitches about 3mm (⅛in) in from the edge of the fabric, working your way across to the dot at B.

3 Remove the fabric from the hoop and press creases from the wrong side of the fabric. The heat from the iron should freshen up the marked outline of the head on the fabric. Re-trace the outline and dot markings onto the wrong side of the fabric. Secure the head fabric and forehead fabric together with pins, pinning from the wrong side of the head fabric.

4 To secure the forehead patch on the head, place the head (wrong side of fabric up) onto the bed of the sewing machine and stitch around the top of the head, beginning at the dot at A and working around to the dot at B, sewing directly onto the marked line.

5 Place an 18cm (7in) square of cotton fabric for the front head right sides together with a 18cm (7in) square of cotton fabric for the head back, and pin together.

6 To complete the head and the rest of the body, refer to the Basic Doll chapter.

4.

5.

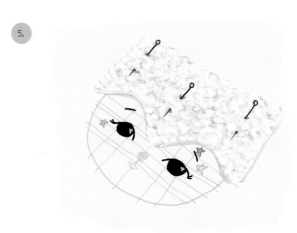

6.

EARS

- 10cm x 7.5cm (4in x 3in) cotton teddy fur for outer ears
- 10cm x 7.5cm (4in x 3in) pink cotton fabric for inner ears
- Machine sewing thread to match outer ears

LAYOUT, CUTTING AND SEWING

1 Place the outer ear fabric and inner ear fabric together, right sides facing. Using a disappearing-ink marker, trace the left and right ear patterns directly onto the cotton fabric, transferring the dots for the opening at the base of the ears (Fig 7). Pin the pieces together. Stitch around each ear, beginning at one dot at the base of the ear and sewing around to the dot on the opposite side, leaving the area between open for turning. Begin and end each seam with a back stitch and leave a long tail of thread at one end for sewing openings closed. Trim excess fabric around each ear, leaving a little tab between the dots for the openings.

2 Turn the ears right side out, tuck the tabs in and ladder stitch the openings closed, leaving a tail of thread for attaching the ears to the head later on. Press, ironing the cotton fabric side of the ear if using teddy fur for the outer ear. Referring to the ear paper pattern piece as a guide, fold each fabric ear over where indicated by the dotted line and then pin. Blanket stitch the sides of the ear together, leaving a tail of thread for attaching the ear to the head (Fig 8).

3 To attach the ears to the head, pin each ear on each side of the head (Fig 9). Ladder stitch the front and the back of each ear onto the head seam.

MAKING THE BODY (IF USING TEDDY FUR)

1 The body can be made with the same fabric that you've used to create the head, arms and legs, or you can make it out of the teddy fur or alternate fabric. Due to the stretchy nature of teddy fur, the seams for the front and back body parts should be sewn a little further away from the edges – about 1.5cm (½in) instead of the 5mm (¼in) given in the main pattern instructions. This will prevent the body from stretching out of proportion once stuffed.

2 Trace the body pattern pieces onto the back of the teddy fur with a disappearing-ink marker and then cut out. I found it easier to hand sew the body pieces together using a back stitch along all seams, and keeping the stitches about 1.5cm (½in) away from the edges, but you could attempt to sew the teddy fur by machine. Once sewn, turn body right side out and begin stuffing, gently directing the stuffing into the neck area, tummy and bottom and taking care not to stretch the fabric as you do so. Stitch the back opening closed.

7.

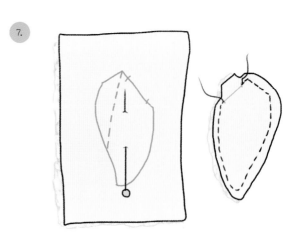

8.

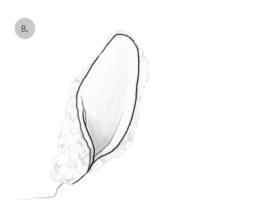

9.

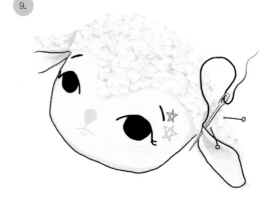

Tip

IF YOU'RE USING TEDDY FUR FABRIC FOR THE OUTER EARS, YOU MAY FIND IT EASIER TO HAND STITCH THE EARS TOGETHER USING A BACK STITCH.

SLEEP TOP

YOU WILL NEED

- 23cm x 18cm (9in x 7in) floral cotton fabric for top
- 23cm x 18cm (9in x 7in) lightweight solid cotton fabric for lining of top
- Machine sewing threads to match top fabric and trim
- One 5mm (¼in) snap closure
- Straw and orange stick or chopstick
- Trim for neckline and hem 5mm (¼in) wide
- Fray Check or fabric glue

LAYOUT, CUTTING AND SEWING

1 Place the floral and solid fabric together, right sides facing. Using a disappearing-ink marker, trace the sleep top pattern directly onto the fabric and then pin the pieces together (Fig 10).

2 Beginning at dot A (see Fig 11), stitch along the side of the back, around the neckline and then down along the opposite back side to the dot at B, sewing directly onto the marked line and starting and ending your seam with a back stitch. Sew up each armhole, beginning at dot C and sewing up around the curve to D (Fig 12). Pin the unsewn sides of the top together to prevent the fabric from shifting and trim excess fabric around the edges, leaving 5mm (¼in) around marked/sewn lines. Notch curves around the neck and armholes, being careful not to cut into the stitches.

3 Remove the pins and turn the top right side out, using a straw and chopstick to aid in turning (Fig 13). Use a chopstick to push out corners (Fig 14) and press (Fig 15).

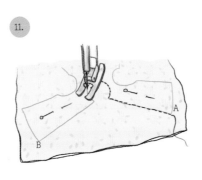

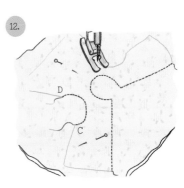

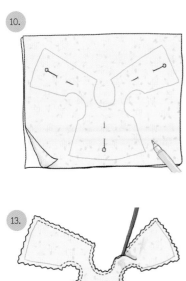

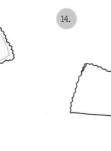

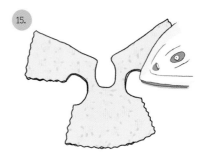

4 With right sides facing, fold the top over at the shoulders, so that the front and back sides match. Pin along the sides (Fig 16). Machine sew the sides, sewing about 5mm (¼in) away from the cut edges of the fabric. Open the seams and press flat. Pin the bottom edges together (Fig 17) and machine sew closed with a small zig-zag stitch.

5 For the trim, measure the width of the bottom and around the neckline and cut trim to match. Run a small bead of Fray Check along the trim's cut edges and allow to dry thoroughly. Pin the trim onto the neckline and hand sew on with one strand of matching thread, keeping stitches small and neat (the thread is shown in a dark colour in Fig 18 in order to be seen).

6 Fold the bottom edge of the top up about 5mm (¼in) and pin. Hand tack (baste) the hem down with one strand of thread. Pin the trim onto the hem (Fig 19). Machine sew in place with matching thread and then remove the tacking (basting) stitches.

7 Fit the top onto the doll and turn it around so that the back of the doll is facing you. Determine where the snap closures should be and mark the area on each side of the back with a disappearing-ink marker. Remove the top and sew the snaps in place.

YOU COULD CONSIDER ADDING TRIM
AROUND THE ARMHOLES OF THE TOP.
TO DO SO, PIN THE TRIM AROUND
THE INSIDE OF THE ARMHOLE AND
THEN HAND STITCH IT IN PLACE.

16.

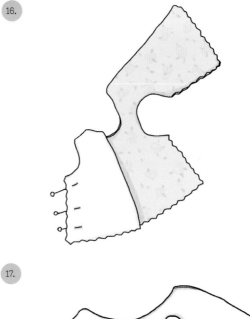

17.

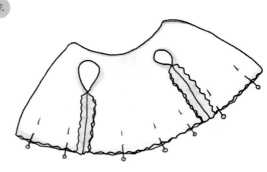

18.

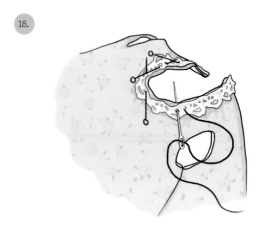

19.

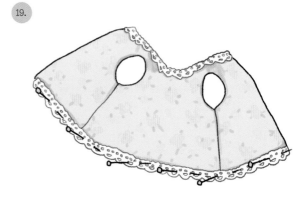

BLOOMERS

- Two pieces 16.5cm x 10cm (6½in x 4in) cotton fabric for bloomers
- Machine sewing thread to match fabric
- Elastic for waistband 5mm (¼in) wide
- Elastic for leg openings 3mm (⅛in) wide
- Two small safety pins for threading elastic

LAYOUT, CUTTING AND SEWING

1 Place the two pieces of fabric together, right sides facing. Pin the bloomers pattern piece onto the fabric and cut out the shape. To mark the casement placement for the elastic around the waistband and the hems on the bottom of each leg opening, remove the pins and separate the front and back fabric pieces, placing them right side up on your work table. Place the paper pattern piece onto one of the fabric pieces, centring it. Carefully lift the outer edges, using a disappearing-ink marker to mark the beginning of the lines on either side of the waistband and leg openings onto the fabric. Repeat on the second piece. Use a ruler and the marker to connect the lines on each fabric piece (Fig 20).

2 Place the bloomers pieces together, right sides facing, and pin together on one side from A to B (see Fig 21). Stitch down from the top edge of the waistband at A and around the curve of the crotch to B, keeping your stitches about 5mm (¼in) from the seam edge. Open the fabric and press the seam flat. Fold the waistband edge and leg openings over (wrong sides facing), using your marked lines as a guide and pin. Stitch the edges down, keeping stitches very close to the cut edge, about 1.5mm–2mm (¹/₁₆in–⅛in) away from cut edge (Fig 22).

3 Cut a piece of 5mm (¼in) wide elastic measuring about 16cm (6¼in) for the waistband. This measurement was perfect for my doll's waist area. However, you may want to measure around the widest area below your doll's waist and add 1.5cm (½in) to the get the perfect measurement for your doll. Pin a small safety pin horizontally onto one end of the elastic, to help guide the elastic through the casing. Pin the second safety pin onto the opposite end, this time pinning it vertically, to help prevent the end of the elastic from slipping through the casing. For the leg openings, I cut two pieces of 3mm (⅛in) wide elastic, each 5.7cm (2¼in). As with the waistband, you can measure around the top of your doll's thigh to make sure that this measurement works for your doll. To sew the elastic onto the leg openings, pin the end of a piece of elastic directly onto the hem stitches of one of the leg openings on the wrong side of the fabric (Fig 23).

20.

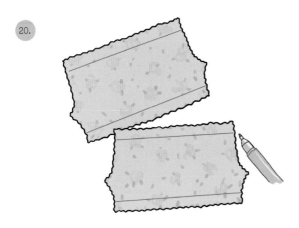

21.

22.

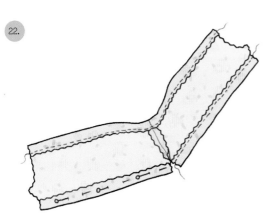

23.

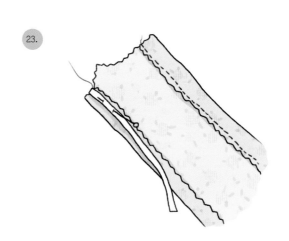

4 Start by securing the end of the elastic onto the hem seam by making four or five back stitches onto the centre of the elastic. This will prevent the elastic from slipping as you sew. Continue stitching the elastic onto the hem seam, carefully stretching the elastic onto the seam with one hand so that it matches the width of the leg opening as you sew, while using your other hand to keep the tension on the fabric as it comes out of the back of the machine foot. Work carefully, keeping the tension of the fabric and elastic even on either end. End with a back stitch at the opposite end. Repeat on second leg opening.

5 Thread the 5mm (¼in) wide elastic through the waistband casing. Pull a 5mm (¼in) tab of elastic out at either end, even out the gathers along the top of the waistband and then secure the elastic in place with straight pins (Fig 24). Remove safety pins. Use a small zig-zag stitch to sew the edges of the seam casing closed (back stitch over the area a couple of times to secure). Snip off excess elastic after sewing.

6 Fold the fabric along the centre seam so that right sides are facing. Pin from the waistband at A around to the crotch at B (Fig 25). Sew in place, keeping your stitches about 5mm (¼in) from the edge. Leave a long tail of thread at the top edge of the seam.

7 To neaten the seam at the back of the waistband and the seams on the leg openings, open and flatten the seams and stitch the edges down onto the fabric on either side. With the right sides of the fabric facing, follow Fig 26, matching the seams at the centre (B) and at the bottom of each leg (C) and pinning. Stitch around the inner leg seam from C to C. Notch around the crotch area and turn right side out. Open and flatten the leg opening seams and stitch the edges down onto the fabric on either side (Fig 27).

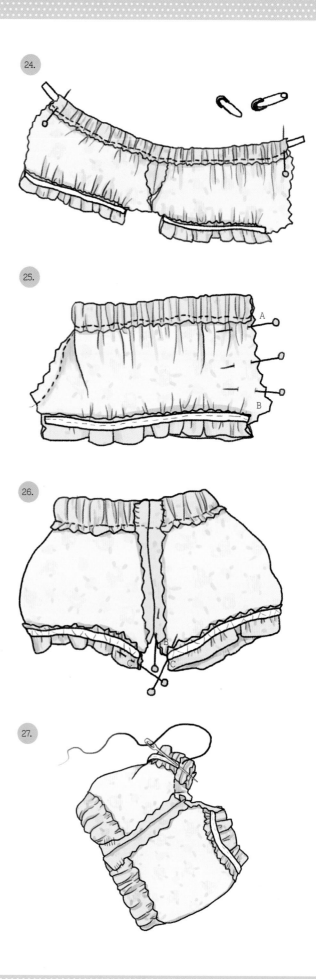

24.

25.

26.

27.

SLEEP MASK

- DMC Cotton embroidery thread (floss): white, black (310) for eyes, medium brown (3863) for snout and light pink (761) for inner ears and for blanket stitching front and back mask pieces together
- 10cm x 12.5cm (4in x 5in) white felt for mask
- Two pieces of ribbon each 5mm x 30.5cm (¼in x 12in)
- 5cm (2in) square yellow felt for bow
- Scraps of pink felt for inner ears
- Pink pencil

LAYOUT, CUTTING AND SEWING

1 Note that the mask is stitched entirely by hand. Pin the sleep mask pattern piece onto white felt and cut out two pieces. Cut out the bow pieces on the yellow felt and the inner ears from the pink felt using a pair of embroidery scissors.

2 To mark the grid for the facial features on the mask, keep the front facing mask pattern piece pinned in place and gently lift the outer edges, using a disappearing-ink marker to mark the beginning of the lines onto the felt. On the back facing side of the mask, only mark the beginning of the horizontal line running through the centre. This will be your guide for positioning the ribbon ties. Remove the pattern piece and use a ruler to connect the lines. Using the mask pattern piece as a guide, transfer the eyes and snout onto the front facing felt piece with a disappearing-ink marker.

3 Pin the ends of each ribbon on either side of the marked line on the back facing piece, overlapping the ribbon edges onto the felt by about 1.5cm (½in). With white embroidery thread, back stitch the overlapping sides of each ribbon onto the mask, beginning and ending your thread on this side of the felt (Fig 28). This will ensure that the stitches (and the overlapping ribbon ends) will be sandwiched between the two layers of felt, keeping them hidden once the front and back of the mask are sewn together. Position the inner ears onto the ears on the front of the mask and stitch in place with small stitches and light pink thread to match inner ears.

4 Using black embroidery thread, outline the curve of the eyelid and lashes on each eye with stem stitch. Outline the snout with medium brown thread and then fill in with satin stitches (Fig 29).

5 To make the bow, follow Fig 30. Fold the bow felt in half widthways. Whip stitch the two short ends together. Re-fold the bow so that the stitches run down the centre. Position the short edge of the bow centre onto the centre of the whip stitches. Whip stitch the short edge onto the centre of the stitches. Wrap the bow centre around over the front of the bow, overlapping the opposite short edge onto the stitched edge. Stitch in place. Pin the bow just below an ear and hand stitch in place.

6 Pin the front of the mask onto the back of the mask (Fig 31). Blanket stitch all the way around. Use a pink pencil to add some colour to the cheeks. Place the mask onto the lamb, tying the ribbons at the back of the head.

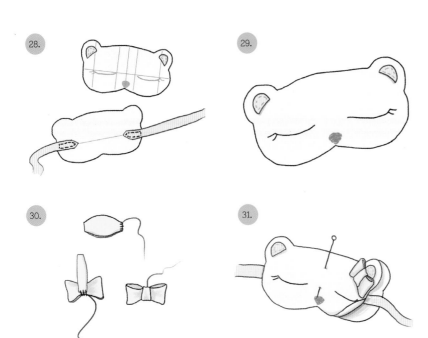

LULLABY LAMB
PATTERNS

The Lamb also requires the Basic Doll patterns – see end of Basic Doll chapter. All the patterns are actual size, so there is no need to enlarge or reduce them. Printable versions of these patterns can be downloaded from: http://ideas.sewandso.co.uk/patterns.

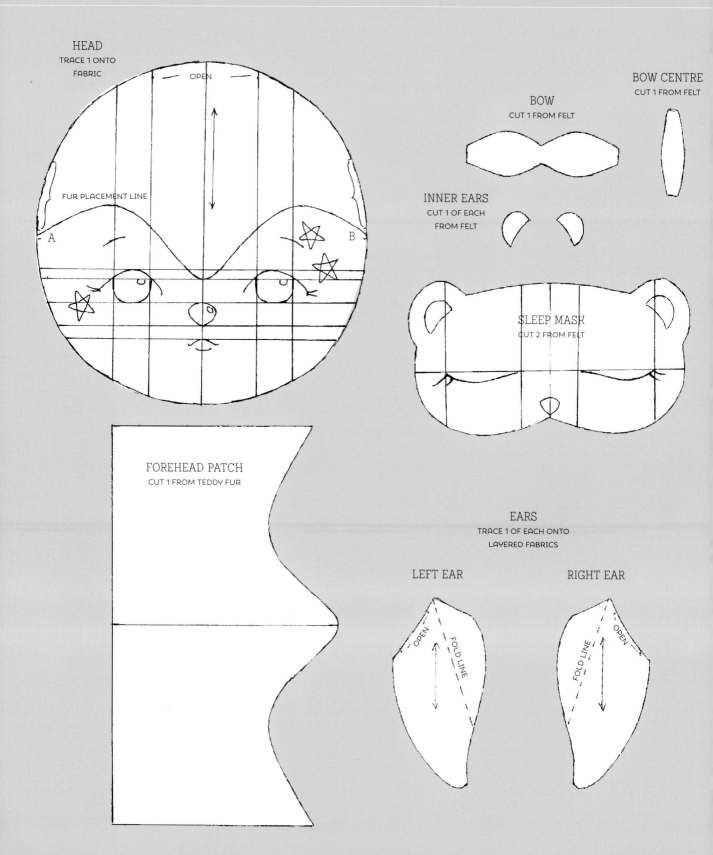

HEAD
TRACE 1 ONTO
FABRIC

OPEN

FUR PLACEMENT LINE

A

B

BOW
CUT 1 FROM FELT

BOW CENTRE
CUT 1 FROM FELT

INNER EARS
CUT 1 OF EACH
FROM FELT

SLEEP MASK
CUT 2 FROM FELT

FOREHEAD PATCH
CUT 1 FROM TEDDY FUR

EARS
TRACE 1 OF EACH ONTO
LAYERED FABRICS

LEFT EAR

OPEN

FOLD LINE

RIGHT EAR

FOLD LINE

OPEN

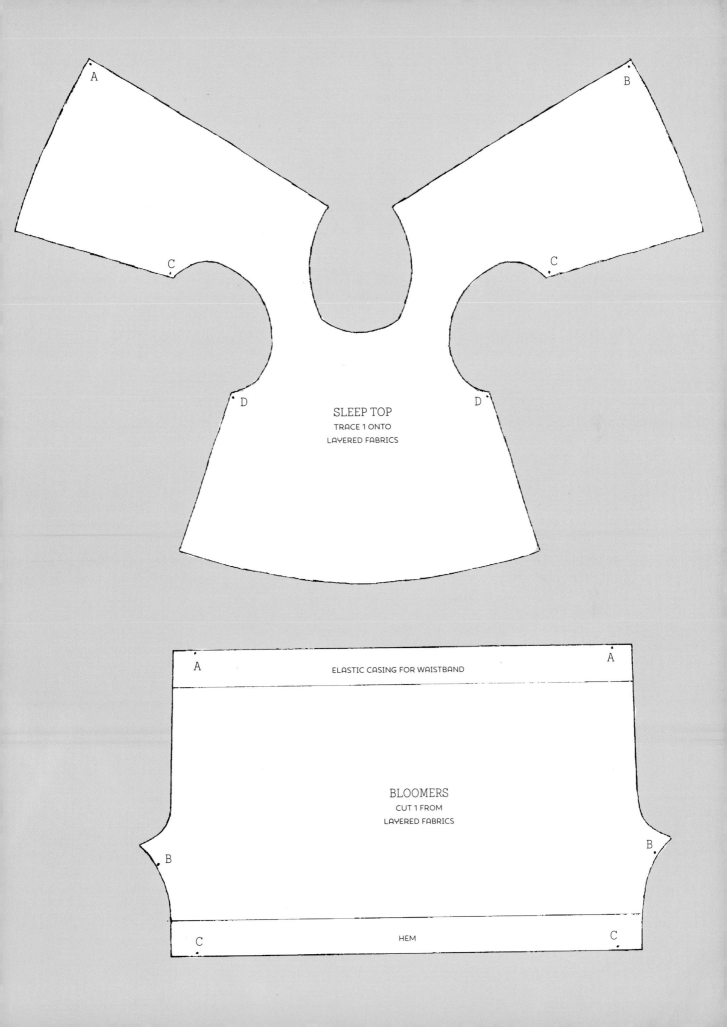

SLEEP TOP
TRACE 1 ONTO
LAYERED FABRICS

A

B

C

C

D

D

ELASTIC CASING FOR WAISTBAND

A

A

BLOOMERS
CUT 1 FROM
LAYERED FABRICS

B

B

HEM

C

C

FANCIFUL
Unicorn

Unicorns are enchanting creatures and this cutie is no exception, especially when carrying her favourite lion doll (see next chapter). With her magical horn and gorgeous flowing mane, she's delightfully charming. She wears an adorable long-sleeved dress edged with a delicate cotton trim and gauzy leg warmers in a glittery mesh fabric.

YOU WILL NEED

FACE AND FLOWER EMBROIDERY

- DMC Cotton embroidery thread (floss): black (310) for eyes and eyebrows, pink (761) for mouth, dark pink (3708) for snout, aqua (964), apricot (352) and lavender (209) for flowers, chartreuse (907) for leaves, pale orange (3854), periwinkle (3811) and light pink (761) for French knots
- DMC Satin embroidery thread: white (S5200) for eye highlights (or white Cotton embroidery thread)
- Embroidery needle
- Disappearing-ink marker, ruler and embroidery hoop

HAND EMBROIDERY STITCHES USED

Refer to the Stitch Guide chapter for these stitches.

- Stem stitch
- Satin stitch
- Straight stitch
- French knot
- Ladder stitch
- Whip stitch
- Running stitch

MAKING THE BASIC DOLL

Refer to the Basic Doll chapter to make the doll and transfer the head facial features and embroidery motifs onto the doll's head. Note that a suede fabric was used for the body and head. Embroider the facial features (eyes and eyebrows) as in the Basic Doll chapter, Embroidering the Facial Features. All embroidery is done with one strand of thread unless otherwise stated.

WORKING THE HEAD EMBROIDERY MOTIFS

1 Use stem stitch to embroider the outline of the snout with dark pink thread and the mouth with pink (Fig 1). To make the French knots at the centre of each flower, use one strand of each colour (pale orange, periwinkle and light pink) for each flower centre, winding the thread around the needle three times to form each knot. Embroider the flower petals for each flower with straight stitches, following the lines on the head pattern, in aqua, apricot and lavender. Use one strand of each of the colours to complete the petals of each flower (Fig 2). Now embroider the leaves with straight stitches using chartreuse thread (Fig 3).

2 To complete the head and the rest of the body, refer to the Basic Doll chapter.

EARS

YOU WILL NEED

- 12.5cm (5in) square cotton fabric to match body
- Matching sewing thread

LAYOUT, CUTTING AND SEWING

1 Fold the fabric in half, right sides facing. Trace the left and right ear patterns directly onto the fabric with a disappearing-ink marker and then transfer the dots for the opening at the base of each ear. Pin the pieces together. Stitch around each ear, beginning at one dot and sewing around to the dot on the opposite side, leaving the area between the dots open for turning. Begin and end each seam with a back stitch and leave a long tail of thread once you've reached the dot on the opposite side, for sewing the openings closed. Trim excess fabric around each ear, leaving a little tab between the dots for the openings (Fig 4). Turn the ears right side out, tuck the tabs in, ladder stitch the openings closed and press.

2 To attach the ears to the head, fold the ears slightly and then pin each ear onto the marked area at the top of the head, referring to the illustration as a guide. Ladder stitch the front and back of each ear onto the head seam (Fig 5).

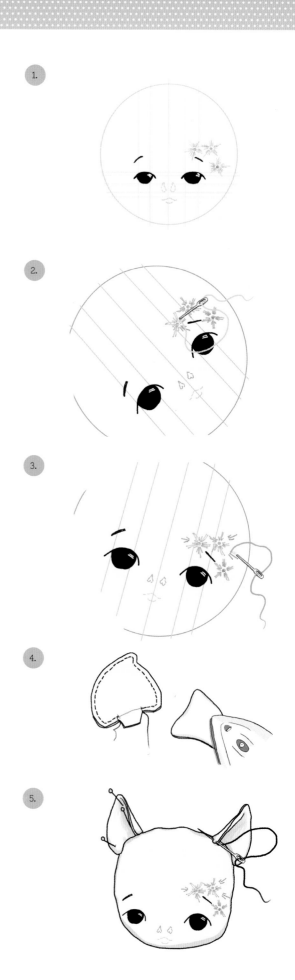

1.

2.

3.

4.

5.

HORN AND MANE

- 10cm x 7.5cm (4in x 3in) fabric for horn
- 10cm (4in) square faux fur fabric for mane
- Sewing threads to match hem and mane
- Small amount of stuffing (fiber fill)
- Small, sharp embroidery scissors
- Cotton bud (Q-tip) for stuffing horn

HORN LAYOUT, CUTTING AND SEWING

1 Fold the fabric in half, right sides facing. Using a disappearing-ink marker, trace the horn pattern directly onto the fabric, transferring the dots for the opening along the side of the horn. Pin the pieces together. Stitch around the horn, beginning at one dot and sewing around to the dot on the opposite side, leaving the area between the dots open for turning and stuffing. Begin and end each seam with a back stitch and leave a long tail of thread once you've reached the dot on the opposite side for sewing the openings closed (Fig 6). Trim excess fabric around the horn, leaving a little tab between the dots for the opening. Turn the horn right side out, tuck the tabs in, ladder stitch the openings closed and press.

2 Fold the horn in half lengthways, pin the edges together and ladder stitch the edges together, beginning at the wider part and ending at the tip (Fig 7). Stuff the horn firmly, packing the stuffing in all the way to the opening with a cotton bud (Q-tip) (Fig 8).

MANE LAYOUT, CUTTING AND SEWING

1 Note that the tiny arrows marked on the faux fur mane pattern pieces show in which direction the fur pile should lay. With a disappearing-ink marker, trace the mane front and back pattern pieces onto the back of the faux fur (the back will look like knit fabric), positioning the arrows marked on the pattern pieces in the same direction as the fur pile (Fig 9). Use a small, sharp pair of scissors to cut out the mane pieces, cutting through the fabric backing only (Fig 10). Keep the nose of the scissors beneath the fur pile, as this will prevent you from snipping into the fur.

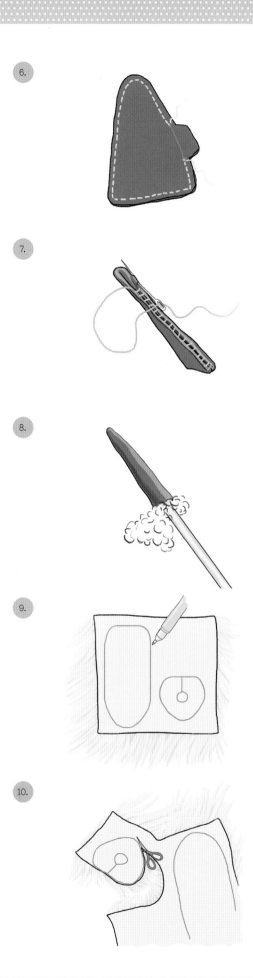

6.

7.

8.

9.

10.

2 Fold the front mane faux fur piece in half, right sides facing and whip stitch along the centre slit (Fig 11). Position the straight edge of the front fur piece onto the head seam, centring it between the ears and onto the forehead and pin in place along the head seam (Fig 12). Carefully move the hair aside so that you can clearly see the cut-out hole in the centre of the fur. Use a disappearing-ink marker to trace the outline of the hole onto the centre of the forehead (Fig 13). Remove the fur and position the horn onto the circle with the seam of the horn facing towards the back of the head. Pin the horn in place and then ladder stitch in place (Fig 14).

3 Reposition the front mane piece onto the forehead, sliding the horn through the hole and pinning the straight edge of the front mane onto the head seam (Fig 15). Centre the front rounded edge of the fur piece down onto the forehead and pin the edges onto the forehead. Stitch the edges of the fur backing down onto the head, using whip stitch and keeping stitches small and neat. Stitch all the way around the entire front fur piece. Repeat this process for the back fur piece, first pinning the straight edge onto the head seam, centring the fur piece down the middle of the back of the head and then whip stitching all the way around.

4 Add a smidgen of colour to your unicorn's mouth and snout with a pink pencil. I found it helpful to pin her hair up and out of the way with a tiny hair clamp before sewing the head to the body (Fig 16).

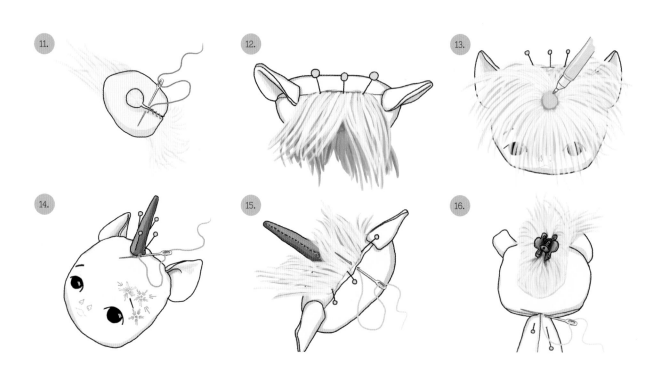

DRESS AND LEGGINGS

YOU WILL NEED

- 10cm (4in) square cotton fabric for neck and sleeve binding
- 46cm x 30.5cm (18in x 12in) cotton fabric in contrasting colour for dress front, dress back and sleeves
- 1.3cm x 30.5cm (½in x 12in) cotton trim for hem
- One 5mm (¼in) snap closure
- 15cm (6in) square stretch glitter netting for leggings
- Machine sewing thread to match fabric
- Embroidery thread in a contrasting colour for hem accent
- Fray Check or fabric glue

DRESS LAYOUT, CUTTING AND SEWING

1 Pin the neck and sleeve binding paper pattern pieces onto the 10cm (4in) square of fabric, placing the arrows on each piece onto the grain of the fabric (Fig 17). These pieces are cut on the bias to create a binding for the neckline and sleeves.

2 Fold the left side of the 46cm x 30.5cm (18in x 12in) fabric over by about 10cm (4in), right sides of fabric facing (Fig 18). Pin the dress back and sleeve onto the doubled side of the fabric, and then pin the dress front onto the remaining fabric. Cut out the pieces.

3 To assemble the dress, begin with the sleeves, sewing two rows of gathering stitches about 5mm (¼in) below the bottom (widest) edge of each sleeve, leaving long threads on either side for pulling up the gathers later (Fig 19). Fold each sleeve in half, using a disappearing-ink marker to mark the centre along the bottom edges on the right side of fabric. Mark the centre of each sleeve binding in the same manner. Match the centre dot on the bottom edge of the sleeve with the centre dot on the top edge of the sleeve binding, right sides facing, and pin at the centre. Now pin the sides of the sleeve to the sides of the binding. Repeat with the second sleeve and binding. Gently pull on the top layer of gathering threads on both sides of each sleeve until the width of the bottom of the sleeve matches the width of the binding. Use the back of a needle to spread the gathers evenly across the edge and then pin.

4 Set your machine stitch on a regular stitch and position the fabric so that the needle is about 5mm (¼in) away from the edge of the sleeve/binding edge. Stitch the binding to the sleeve and then remove gathering threads. Press the seam upwards (Fig 20). Fold the binding around the bottom edge of the sleeve and onto the wrong side of the fabric and pin. Hand stitch the binding onto the seam.

5 With the right sides of the fabric facing, pin the sleeves onto the dress front, matching armholes (Fig 21). Sew together, about 5mm (¼in) away from the armhole edges. Press the seams open. Pin the sleeves to the dress backs, matching armholes (Fig 22). Sew together and press seams open.

6 Sew two rows of gathering stitches about 5mm (¼in) below the edge of the neckline of the dress, leaving long threads on either side for pulling up the gathers later. Mark the centre of the neckline on the right side of the fabric with a disappearing-ink marker. Mark the centre of the neck binding in the same manner. Match the centre dot of the neck binding with the centre dot on the neckline of the dress, right sides facing, and pin at the centre. Pin the left-hand side edge of the binding to the left-hand side edge of the dress, and then pin the right-hand side edge of the binding to the right-hand side edge of the dress. Gently pull the gathers on each side of the neckline until the width of the neckline matches the width of the binding, pinning along the top edge (Fig 23). To ensure that your gathers are even, use the back of a large needle to spread the gathers evenly across the neckline. Sew the binding to the neckline, stitching about 5mm (¼in) away from the edge. Remove the gathering threads. Press the seam upwards. Fold the binding around the neckline and onto the wrong side of the fabric and pin (Fig 24). Hand stitch the binding onto the seam.

7 Fold the long straight sides of the dress backs in on either side of the fabric about 5mm (¼in), wrong sides facing, and pin (Fig 25). Machine sew the folded edges down on either side. With the right sides facing, pin the sides of the dress front to the sides of the dress backs. Sew the side seams together, beginning at the edge of the sleeve binding and stitching all around the sleeves, armholes and sides of the dress (Fig 26). Leave a tail of thread at the beginning of each arm seam. Notch curves around each armhole making sure not to snip into the stitches. Open the seams and press flat.

23.

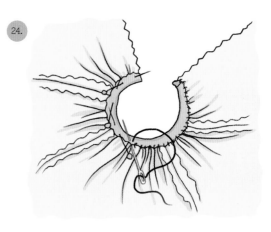

24.

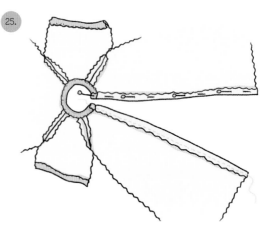

25.

26.

8 To neaten the opening of the sleeves, flatten the seam at each arm opening and use the tail of machine thread to stitch each side of the seam down onto the binding, being careful to stitch onto the top layer of the fabric, so your stitches aren't visible from the right side of the fabric (Fig 27).

9 Turn the dress right side out and sew the snap closure in place at the neck. Fold the bottom edge of the dress up about 5mm (¼in) to create a hem and pin (Fig 28). For the trim, measure the width of the bottom of the skirt and cut trim to match. Run a small bead of Fray Check or fabric glue along the trim's cut edges and allow to dry thoroughly. This will help prevent the ends from fraying. Pin the trim onto the hem on the wrong side of the fabric (Fig 29). Hand sew the trim in place with one or two rows of small running stitches in a contrasting embroidery thread.

MAKING THE LEGGINGS

1 Fold the left edge of the stretch glitter netting to the centre of the fabric and then pin the leggings paper pattern piece on the fold and cut out. Fold the remaining fabric in half widthways and cut out a second legging piece. Fold the short sides of each legging over about 5mm (¼in), wrong sides facing, and pin (Fig 30). Machine sew the folded edges down. Fold each legging in half lengthways, right sides facing, and pin. Machine sew one long edge about 5mm (¼in) away from the cut edge.

2 Turn the leggings right sides out. You'll notice that one end of each piece is slightly wider than the other. Slide the doll's foot into the widest end and position the seam so that it runs up the back of the leg. Gently scrunch the leggings for a slouchy look.

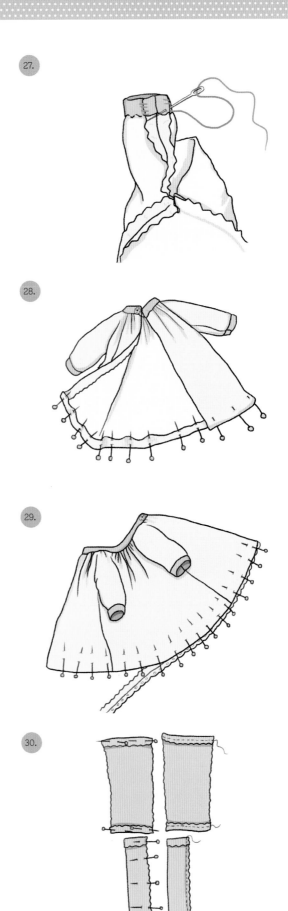

27.

28.

29.

30.

FANCIFUL UNICORN PATTERNS

The Unicorn also requires the Basic Doll patterns – see end of Basic Doll chapter. All the patterns are actual size, so there is no need to enlarge or reduce them. Printable versions of these patterns can be downloaded from: http://ideas.sewandso.co.uk/patterns.

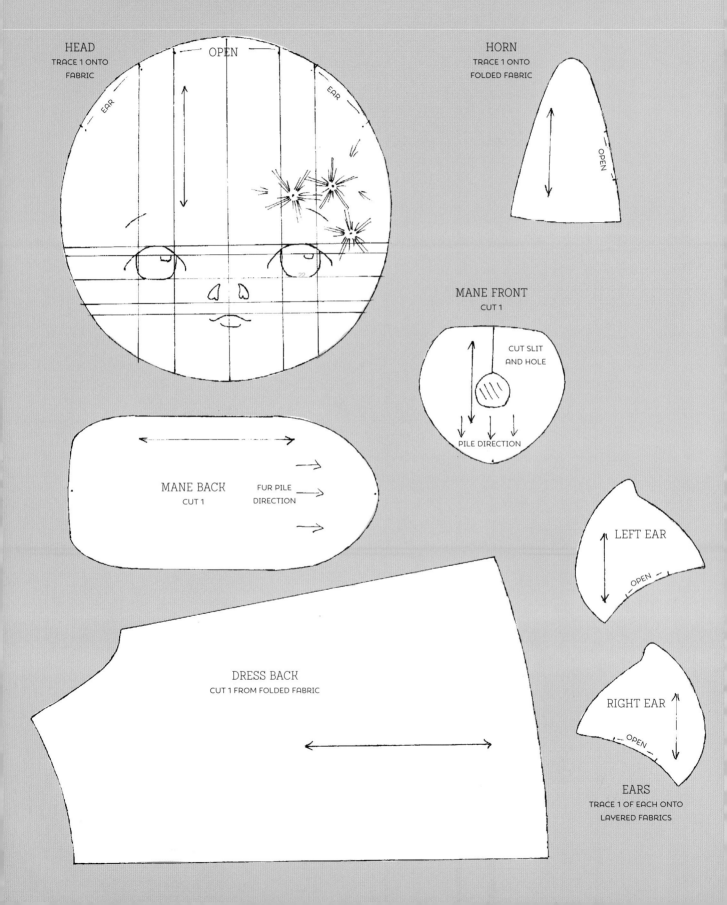

HEAD
TRACE 1 ONTO FABRIC

OPEN

EAR

EAR

22

HORN
TRACE 1 ONTO FOLDED FABRIC

OPEN

MANE FRONT
CUT 1

CUT SLIT AND HOLE

PILE DIRECTION

MANE BACK
CUT 1

FUR PILE DIRECTION

LEFT EAR

OPEN

RIGHT EAR

OPEN

DRESS BACK
CUT 1 FROM FOLDED FABRIC

EARS
TRACE 1 OF EACH ONTO LAYERED FABRICS

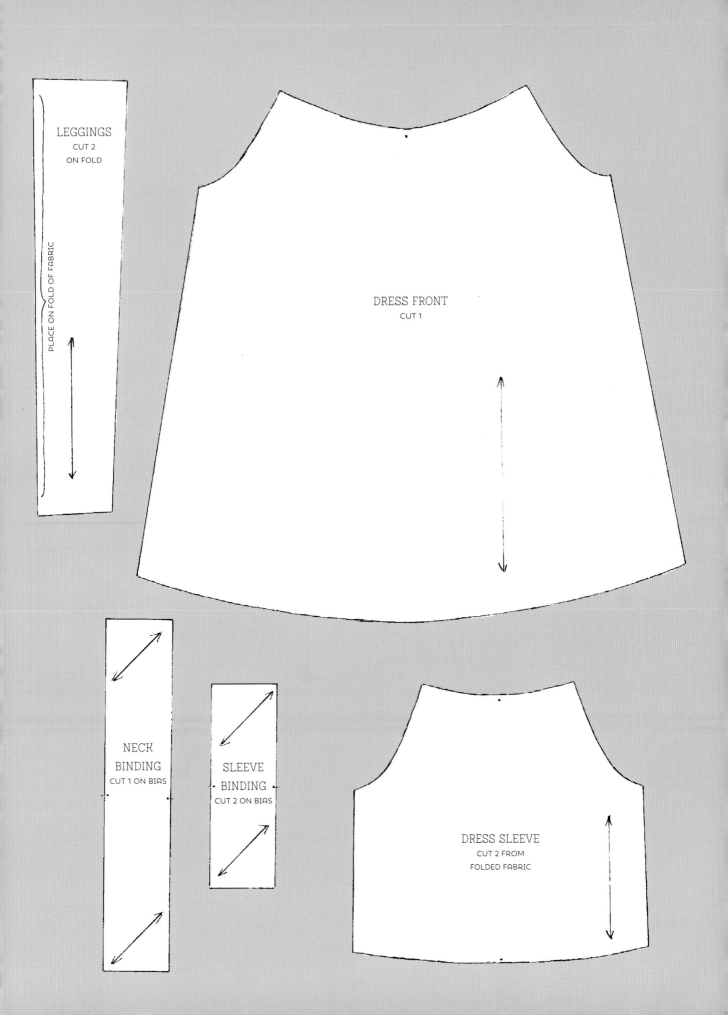

LEGGINGS
CUT 2
ON FOLD

PLACE ON FOLD OF FABRIC

DRESS FRONT
CUT 1

NECK
BINDING
CUT 1 ON BIAS

SLEEVE
BINDING
CUT 2 ON BIAS

DRESS SLEEVE
CUT 2 FROM
FOLDED FABRIC

LI'L Lion

This adorable baby lion doll is stitched by hand and made from wool felt. It would be perfect as a toy for the larger dolls. He could also be made into a hanging ornament simply by stitching a loop of narrow ribbon onto his head – a lovely idea if you'd like to make a gift for someone special!

YOU WILL NEED

- 15cm x 23cm (6in x 9in) wool felt in tan for lion's head, body, arms and ears
- 2.5cm x 18cm (1in x 7in) pale blue wool felt for mane
- Scraps of wool felt in light pink, medium pink, dark pink and brown for muzzle, cheeks, heart patch and snout respectively
- DMC Cotton embroidery thread (floss): tan (3864) for body, brown (3862) for snout and eyebrows, pale blue (747) for mane, baby pink (963) for cheeks, muzzle and heart patch
- Embroidery needle
- A pair of 6mm (¼in) safety eyes
- Disappearing-ink marker and ruler
- Stuffing (fiber fill)
- Stuffing tools such as a chopstick or orange stick and a cotton bud (Q-tip) with one end cut off (for stuffing arms)
- Awl (or sharp, long-nosed embroidery scissors)
- Flat-headed screwdriver and wire cutters (optional)
- Pink pencil

HAND EMBROIDERY STITCHES USED

Refer to the Stitch Guide chapter for these stitches.

- Whip stitch
- Straight stitch
- Running stitch
- Ladder stitch
- Blanket stitch
- Appliqué stitch

LAYOUT, CUTTING AND SEWING

1 I've used one strand of embroidery thread to stitch all seams and to attach cheeks, muzzle, snout and heart patch. Trace the pattern pieces onto paper, cut them out and pin each piece onto your chosen felts. Carefully cut around the patterns, using dressmaking scissors to cut out the larger pieces and embroidery scissors to cut out the smaller ones.

2 To mark the grid lines on the front of the head, keep the head pattern piece pinned in place and gently lift its outer edges, using a disappearing-ink marker to mark the beginning of the lines onto the felt. Remove the pattern piece and use a ruler to connect the lines onto the felt. These markings will help with placement of the lion's facial features. Transfer the markings onto the muzzle and snout.

3 To make the head, use the head pattern piece as a guide, transferring the eye markings onto the front felt head piece with a disappearing-ink marker. Position the felt cheeks on the face and stitch in place. Centre the felt muzzle on the face and stitch in place.

4 Position the snout and stitch in place (Fig 1). Embroider a tiny line down from the base of the snout and onto the muzzle in brown thread. Do not end off the thread. Use a disappearing-ink marker to mark the freckles on either side of the muzzle and then stitch them with the same thread used to stitch on the snout, making a tiny stitch for each freckle.

5 Use an awl (or the tip of long-nosed embroidery scissors) to make a tiny hole for each eye (Fig 2). Insert a safety eye and its connector at the back, making sure to slide the washer (connector) down firmly onto the post as far as it will go. Depending on the type of washer that is used, you may need to open the tiny prongs with the aid of a flat-headed screwdriver before securing the washer onto the post. Once secured on the post, use the screwdriver to push the prongs back down as far as they'll go. This will prevent the washer from sliding off, thus loosening the eye. If desired at this stage, once you've connected the eye parts, you could trim the plastic posts at the back of each eye with a pair of wire cutters, leaving 3mm (⅛in) of post remaining beyond the washer. Using brown thread, stitch each eyebrow with a long straight stitch.

6 Fold each head piece in half, right sides facing and whip stitch the darts at the top of the head from the wrong side of the felt (Fig 3). Place the head front onto the head back, wrong sides together, and pin. Starting at the top of the head, whip stitch all the way around, leaving an opening between the dots for stuffing. Stuff the head firmly and whip stitch the opening closed, adding more stuffing to round out the top of the head as you close the hole. The face should be full and rounded and quite firm, but not to the point of bursting at the seams.

7 To make the ears, whip stitch around the sides of the ears and then blanket stitch the bottom of each ear closed (Fig 4). Pin the ears onto the head seam where indicated on the pattern and ladder stitch the front and back of each ear in place.

8 To make the body, position the heart patch onto the front of the body and stitch in place. Place the front body onto the back body, wrong sides facing, and whip stitch around the body, starting at one side of the neck. Stop about mid body on the opposite side and add stuffing to the legs. Continue whip stitching up to the neck. Stuff the rest of the body firmly. Run a tiny gathering stitch just below the top edge of the neck opening (Fig 5). Gently tighten the thread to close the hole, adding more stuffing to fill up the neck area as needed. Hand stitch closed. You should end up with a tight, rounded nub (Fig 6).

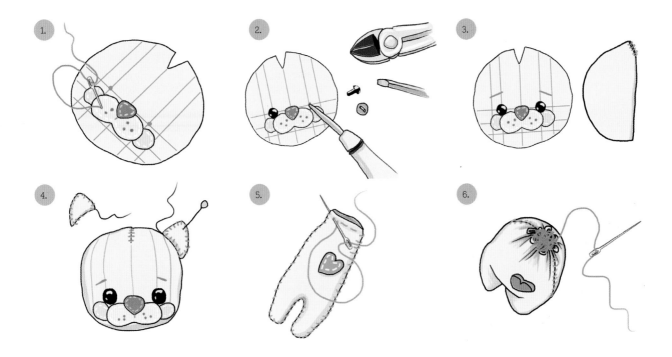

9 To make the arms, pin the arms onto the body, placing the shoulders onto the seams along the side of the body and positioning the lower part of the arms so that they curve around the lion's tummy. Pin in place. Insert a needle threaded with matching embroidery thread in through the centre of the neck and out through the top of the shoulder, about 2mm (⅛in) away from the edge. Keeping your stitches small and neat, appliqué the arms directly onto the body, leaving a small area open for stuffing at the back of the arm (Fig 7). Cut the cotton bud off at one end of a cotton bud (Q-tip) and use the cut end as a stuffing tool to stuff the arm. Stitch the remainder of the arm onto the body.

10 To sew the head to the body, pin the head onto the neck (Fig 8). Ladder stitch around once and then, on the next few rounds, take the ladder stitch a teeny bit lower down onto the neck and a teeny bit higher onto the face. This will bring the head closer onto the neck and make the head more stable. Keep your ladder stitches tiny and straight, as this will give a clean finish to the seam.

11 To make the mane, stitch a line of tiny running stitches along the length of the mane, about 1.5mm (¹/₁₆in) away from the mane's straight edge, keeping a tail of thread attached for attaching the mane onto the head later (Fig 9). Gently gather the thread until the width of the mane matches the circumference of the lion's head (Fig 10). Pin the mane onto the head seam, centring the marked dot in the centre of the mane onto the dart seam at the top of the head, and the short end (knotted thread end) just below the muzzle. Pin the opposite short end (tail of thread end) next to the first end, just below the muzzle, adjusting the gathers as needed to fit the circumference of the head. Secure with more pins. Ladder stitch the mane onto the head seam (Fig 11).

12 As a finishing touch to your little lion, add a bit of colour to the inner ears with a pink pencil (Fig 12).

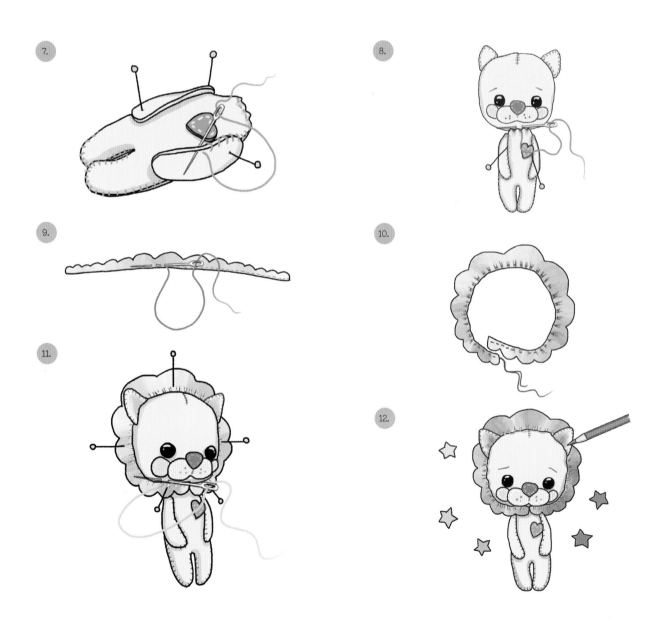

LI'L LION
PATTERNS

All the patterns are actual size, so there is no need to enlarge or reduce them. Printable
versions of these patterns can be downloaded from: http://ideas.sewandso.co.uk/patterns.

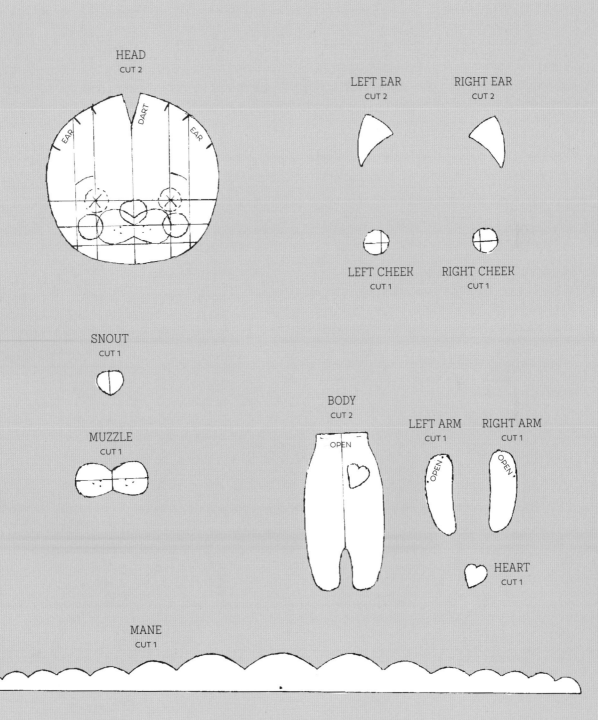

HEAD
CUT 2

LEFT EAR
CUT 2

RIGHT EAR
CUT 2

LEFT CHEEK
CUT 1

RIGHT CHEEK
CUT 1

SNOUT
CUT 1

MUZZLE
CUT 1

BODY
CUT 2

LEFT ARM
CUT 1

RIGHT ARM
CUT 1

HEART
CUT 1

MANE
CUT 1

STITCH GUIDE

For the projects in this book, all of the facial features and embroidered accents are designed to be stitched by hand using easy embroidery stitches as specified in the project instructions. If you've never hand stitched or embroidered before, I recommend that you practise each stitch on a scrap of fabric first. To ensure a nice clean finish to your work, keep your stitches small, neat and evenly spaced. Once you feel confident in your ability to stitch, you'll be ready to start making the dolls. If you require more help, there are plenty of tutorials available online.

LAZY DAISY STITCH

This is also called detached chain stitch. It is an isolated stitch usually worked around in a circle to create the look of flower petals. Used as a single stitch, it can create little leaves.

Bring the needle through to the front of the fabric at the top of the marked line at A on the diagram. Insert the needle right back into the spot at A and bring it out through the front at B, looping the thread under the point of the needle. Pull the thread so that the loop lies flat. Make a very short stitch over the loop and insert the needle down at C to anchor it. Bring the needle out through to the top of the next marked line at A and repeat the process, going around until you've completed the flower.

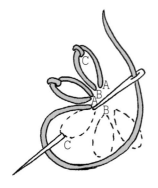

STRAIGHT, RUNNING AND GATHERING STITCHES

These stitches are all basically made using the same technique. When used as a running stitch, the stitches should all be of even length, as should the spaces between the stitches.

A basic straight stitch can be used to make little eyelashes or eyebrows. Running stitches are usually made along a straight or curved line with even spaces between the stitches. Gathering stitches are made in the same manner as running stitches, but the thread is pulled firmly to create a gathered effect on the fabric, ribbon, seam binding or trim.

Insert the threaded needle up from the back of the fabric at A on the diagram and then insert the needle down into the fabric at B. Bring the needle back up a stitch length ahead of B and insert again at C, and so on.

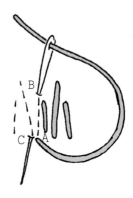

BLANKET STITCH

This simple linear stitch is mostly used to decorate fabric edges.

Bring a threaded needle out through A. Insert the needle at B and bring it out again at C. Keeping the yarn under the needle, pull the thread gently so it's taut, forming a right angle. Insert the needle at D, keeping the thread under the needle as you bring it out at E, and so on.

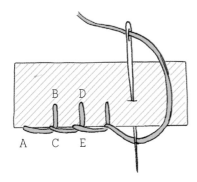

LADDER STITCH

The ladder stitch, also called blind or hidden stitch, is mainly used to close an opening or join two pieces such as the head and the body. The stitch is worked back and forth along the edges of the head and neck where they meet, catching a tiny bit of each side. When pulled tight, the thread will create an invisible seam.

Bring a needle out through A. Insert the needle at B and out through C. Insert the needle at D and out through E, and so on. Every now and then, gently pull the thread taut as this will make the stitches disappear. Keep your stitches tiny, straight and even as you work.

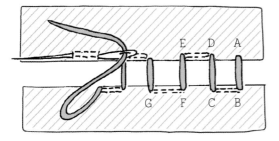

WHIP STITCH

This is a basic stitch that is used to sew two edges of felt or fabric together.

Insert the needle through the wrong side of one piece of felt or fabric and out through the right side at A. Insert the needle at B, on the other piece of fabric, taking it through both layers and out the opposite side at C. Continue stitching in this manner, sewing both edges of the fabric together.

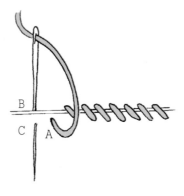

APPLIQUÉ STITCH

An appliqué stitch is usually used to attach a smaller piece of felt or fabric onto a larger one.

Start by positioning the smaller piece where it's needed. Insert the needle from the back of the felt at A on the diagram. Go down into B, come up again at C and so on until you've stitched the smaller piece into place.

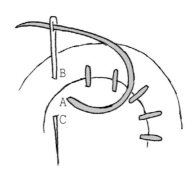

SATIN STITCH

Satin stitch is mostly used to fill in an area, sort of like colouring within the lines in a children's colouring book. The technique is simple, but it is helpful to practise it a few times to achieve perfect results. Basic satin stitch is made by working straight stitches close together in parallel lines.

Bring a threaded needle up through at A, insert into B, come up again at C and so on until you've filled the area. It's important to keep the tension even throughout as this will give a smooth, satin look to the area.

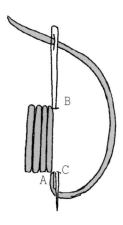

STEM STITCH

Stem stitch, also known as the outline stitch, produces a slightly raised, solid line. It is perfect for outlining areas such as eyes, snout and eyebrows, and is also used throughout the book to outline curves and create straight lines.

Bring the needle out through A. Insert the needle at B, and holding the thread down with your thumb, come up through C halfway between A and B. Let go of the thread under your thumb and gently pull the thread taut. Continue in this pattern, keeping your stitches small and neat.

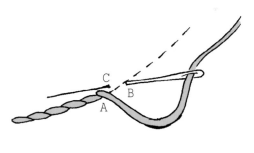

BACK STITCH

This is a similar stitch to stem stitch that makes a finer, slightly raised line, which is good for outlines and details.

Bring a threaded needle up through A and insert at B to make a straight stitch. Come back up at C and go down again at A to make a second straight stitch. Bring the needle up a stitch length ahead of C, then insert down at C, and so on.

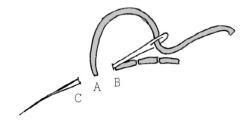

Tip

EMBROIDERING SATIN STITCH MAY BE QUITE
INTIMIDATING AT FIRST, SO IF YOU'VE NEVER
TRIED IT BEFORE, PRACTISE ON A SCRAP
OF FABRIC FIRST. KEEP YOUR STITCHES AS
CLOSE TOGETHER AS POSSIBLE WITHOUT
BUNCHING THEM. WORK SLOWLY AND
METHODICALLY, KEEPING THE TENSION OF
THE THREAD EVEN AS YOU FILL IN EACH AREA.
THIS WILL ENSURE THAT YOUR STITCHES
APPEAR EVENLY SPACED, NEAT AND FLAT.

FRENCH KNOT

A French knot produces a small tight knot that works well for creating a slightly raised stitch to add dimension to your work. They're perfect for creating flower centres and adding a dot of colour here and there. For larger knots you can use more strands of thread.

Bring a threaded needle out through A. Wrap the thread around the needle two or three times. Holding the thread firmly, insert the needle down in to the fabric very near to where you brought it up at A. Hold onto the thread firmly as you slide the needle out through the back of the fabric and pull the knot snug.

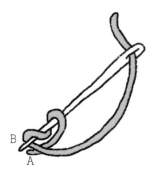

WOVEN WHEEL STITCH

This stitch is also known as spider stitch, and is a beautiful easy-to-embroider stitch, which can be used to create pretty roses in a two-stage process – first the spokes and then the wheel.

Follow the three-stage diagram here and start by creating a five-pointed star using four strands of embroidery thread. Bring the needle up through the back of the fabric at A and into the centre at B. Bring the needle back up through C and down again through B. Continue stitching each spoke of the star, working around in a clockwise manner. Finish by inserting the needle into the centre of the star and out through the back of the fabric. Now begin weaving by bringing the needle up and out through the front of the fabric, very close to the centre and then weaving the thread over and under the stitches in a clockwise direction until your rose is complete.

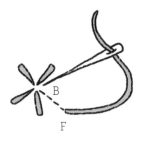

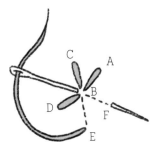

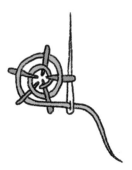

ACKNOWLEDGMENTS

Thank you to the most wonderful team at F&W Media who have contributed to the making of this book. This exciting adventure would not have been possible without your help and guidance! Special thanks to Ame Verso and Sarah Callard for believing in me and allowing me to pour my creative juices into this book and to Linda Clements for the fabulous job she's done editing the book. Many thanks to Sam Staddon for designing the gorgeous layout of the book, Prudence Rogers for her delightful illustrations and Jason Jenkins for the beautiful photographs! I am grateful, too, to Jeni Hennah, Anna Wade and Beverley Richardson – I am very blessed to work with such an amazing team.

To my wonderful Mum, who has been such a huge help running my Etsy shop while I've been writing this book, and to my dear hubby John, whose help on every level has been invaluable – thank you both so much! I am so blessed that you have stood behind me every step of the way!

ABOUT THE AUTHOR

I live in beautiful British Columbia, Canada, in the lovely historical city of New Westminster, with my hubby of 24 years. Our sunny flat overlooks the Fraser River and the Strait of Georgia, beyond which we can see the mountain ranges on Vancouver Island. My 'studio' is really a tiny corner in our dining room, filled with stacks of felt and fabric, pattern pieces, odd buttons and bits and pieces of pretty trim.

SELLING THE DESIGNS

YOU ARE WELCOME TO MAKE AND SELL ANY OF THESE DOLLS, AS LONG AS YOU MENTION THAT YOU HAVE USED A GINGERMELON PATTERN FROM THIS BOOK IN ANY WRITTEN DESCRIPTION OF THE ITEM BEING SOLD. MASS PRODUCTION IS PROHIBITED.

SUPPLIERS

Most of the materials and supplies needed to make the projects in this book can be found at general fabric and craft stores. There are also many online suppliers that carry a wide range of fabrics, trims and sewing supplies if you're unable to find what you need locally.

GINGERMELON DOLLS

www.etsy.com/ca/shop/Gingermelon

My online Etsy shop has additional doll and toy patterns, pattern kits, embroidery templates and paper doll prints created by me. I also carry a large selection of pure merino felts, wool blend felts, printed felts, sewing supplies, safety eyes, embroidery scissors and thread.

ETSY

www.etsy.com

This is an online marketplace where artists can sell their handmade goods. It's great for finding supplies and fabrics such as faux fur and teddy fur.

MICHAELS

www.michaels.com

Stocks embroidery threads, stuffing, craft glue, seed beads, buttons and so on.

JOANN

www.joann.com

For fabrics, faux fur, craft supplies and so on.

SEWANDSO

www.sewandso.co.uk

For fabrics, embroidery threads, craft supplies and so on.

INDEX

A SEWANDSO BOOK
© F&W Media International, Ltd 2019

SewandSo is an imprint of F&W Media International, Ltd
Pynes Hill Court, Pynes Hill, Exeter, EX2 5AZ, UK

F&W Media International, Ltd is a subsidiary of F+W Media, Inc
10151 Carver Road, Suite #200, Blue Ash, OH 45242, USA

Text and Designs © Shelly Down 2019
Layout and Photography © F&W Media International, Ltd 2019

First published in the UK and USA in 2019

A catalogue record for this book is available from the British Library.

ISBN-13: 978-1-4463-0730-4 paperback
SRN: R9321 paperback

ISBN-13: 978-1-4463-7754-3 PDF
SRN: R9953 PDF

ISBN-13: 978-1-4463-7753-6 EPUB
SRN: R9952 EPUB

Printed in China by RR Donnelley for:
F&W Media International, Ltd
Pynes Hill Court, Pynes Hill, Exeter, EX2 5AZ, UK

10 9 8 7 6 5 4 3 2 1

Content Director: Ame Verso
Acquisitions Editor: Sarah Callard
Managing Editor: Jeni Hennah
Project Editor: Lin Clements
Proofreader: Cheryl Brown
Design Manager: Anna Wade
Designer: Sam Staddon
Photographer: Jason Jenkins
Art Direction and Illustration: Prudence Rogers
Production Manager: Beverley Richardson

F&W Media publishes high quality books on a wide range of subjects.
For more great book ideas visit: www.sewandso.co.uk

Layout of the digital edition of this book may vary depending on reader hardware and display settings.